THE JOINT STOCK BOOK
The Making of a Theatre Collective

C000142467

The Joint Stock Theatre Group are the originato
alternative theatre as David Hare's *Fanshen*, Ba
My Masters, *The Ragged Trousered Philanthro*
Lowe, and Caryl Churchill's *Cloud Nine* and *Fe.......... .... working method is
truly innovative and has been much imitated. Their organisational structure
attempts to give the individual company member, whether actor, designer or
administrator, a unique part in the creative process of play-making.

Including a long essay on Joint Stock's work by the volume's editor, Rob
Ritchie, a full, illustrated chronology of all the productions since it was
founded in 1974, and diverse contributions from members past and present,
this book aims to explain the Group's workshop methods, to chronicle the
work itself, and to draw on the experiences and memories of the actors,
writers and directors who have worked with this pioneering and influential
theatre collective over the years.

*The photograph on the front cover is by John Haynes and shows Jennie
Stoller, Amelda Brown and Tricia Kelly in Joint Stock's production of* Fen.

A METHUEN THEATREFILE
in series with

OTHER SPACES: NEW THEATRE AND THE RSC
by Colin Chambers

THE IMPROVISED PLAY: THE WORK OF MIKE LEIGH
by Paul Clements

THE PLAYS OF EDWARD BOND
by Tony Coult

ALL TOGETHER NOW: AN ALTERNATIVE VIEW OF
THEATRE AND THE COMMUNITY
by Steve Gooch

HOW THE VOTE WAS WON: AND OTHER SUFFRAGETTE PLAYS
an anthology, introduced and edited by
Carole Hayman and Dale Spender

PEACE PLAYS
an anthology, introduced and edited by Stephen Lowe

DARIO FO: PEOPLE'S COURT JESTER
by Tony Mitchell

UNDERSTUDIES: THEATRE AND SEXUAL POLITICS
by Michelene Wandor

PLAYS BY WOMEN: VOLUMES ONE–FOUR
a series of anthologies, introduced and edited by Michelene Wandor

PLAYS BY WOMEN: VOLUME FIVE
an anthology, introduced and edited by Mary Remnant

GAY PLAYS: VOLUMES ONE & TWO
anthologies, introduced and edited by Michael Wilcox

THE JOINT STOCK BOOK

THE MAKING OF A THEATRE COLLECTIVE

Edited and introduced by

ROB RITCHIE

A Methuen Paperback

A METHUEN PAPERBACK

First published as a paperback original in 1987
by Methuen London Ltd, 11 New Fetter Lane, London EC4P 4EE
and Methuen Inc, 29 West 35th Street, New York, NY 10001

British Library Cataloguing in Publication Data

The Joint stock book: the making of a
   theatre collective. — (A Methuen
   theatrefile) .
   1. Joint Stock Theatre Group — History
   I. Ritchie, Rob
   792'.022   PN2581

ISBN 0-413-41030-7

Printed in Great Britain by
Hazell, Watson & Viney Ltd
Member of the BPCC Group
Aylesbury, Bucks

CONTENTS

Preface   7

Part One   Joint Stock: 'asking basic questions'   9

Part Two   Productions: an illustrated chronology   33

Part Three   Self-report: notes, essays, adventures   97

PREFACE

The original idea was for a book to mark Joint Stock's tenth birthday in 1984. The birthday came and went, *Fanshen* was not revived, the sequel *Shenfan* was not attempted and the book did not appear. Joint Stock is not a company easily given to celebration. There was a feeling that an illustrated record of the first ten years somehow implied the next ten were in jeopardy. There is some sense in this. We live in an age of the sponsorship brochure and its secret companion the Arts Council hit list. Treading the line between flashy self-publicity and lethal self-criticism is not easy. It was decided to call in an outsider. I was asked to devise a book.

I have never worked for Joint Stock or attended any of their workshops. My only professional encounter with the company was when as an associate director of the Royal Court Theatre, I discussed a co-production contract for *Victory* with Joint Stock's administrator. As I recall it, I spent most of the meeting attempting to conceal a framed certificate awarded to the Royal Court for its production of *Borderline*, a deception prompted by a last minute realisation that *Borderline* had been – as *Victory* was to be – a co-production with Joint Stock. As the newly hung certificate made no mention of this fact, and the accompanying cheque had long been banked, it seemed sensible to hide it. So I stood, I leaned against the wall, I made distracting gestures as I politely insisted the Court's contribution to *Victory* be properly credited in the billings.

I am a little surprised, therefore, to find myself some years later as Joint Stock's official historian. There was no brief given. Privately, I was encouraged by some to do a hatchet job; by others to avoid 'going on and on about *Fanshen*'. In the end, it seemed best to allow Joint Stock's many members to speak for themselves. An editorial committee was formed, a production list drawn up, articles solicited from anyone who wished to contribute. The final selection of material, however, is mine alone and I have tried not to stand in the way of any credits due to the company and its creators.

Rob Ritchie
February 1986

PART ONE
JOINT STOCK
'ASKING BASIC QUESTIONS'

'Asking basic questions' (*Fanshen*, Act I)

It is hard to imagine a more foolish ambition than creating a theatre company, let alone one that tours new plays. The attempt has been known to have ruinous consequences: several people who have tried in the past now live quietly abroad; many are alcoholics; and I know of one psychotherapist who completely redecorated her waiting-room with fees paid by an aspiring artistic director. The company was to have been called 'Bang'. All that remains of this troubled vision is ten square metres of fitted oatmeal in a back room in Maida Vale. Others have not been so lucky.

The attempt, of course, is not often made these days. The idealism that prompted an earlier generation to risk all for a play has vanished – gone, some would say, to try its luck in the British film industry. What remains of that extraordinary upsurge of talent and energy is a dense network of theatre groups, built, staffed and moulded during a decade of expansion that began some time in the mid-sixties. Joint Stock is one of a handful of groups that emerged towards the end of this period. It has a reputation for ensemble work of the highest order, a certain notoriety for long company meetings (eight hours has been claimed though it probably seemed longer) and – rarest of all – it has established a unique approach to making plays: the Joint Stock method.

First, though, there is the work itself. Since it began in 1974, the company has mounted an impressive list of more than twenty productions, ranging through a variety of subjects and styles, from the freewheeling eccentrics of Speakers' Corner to the bleak, flat landscape of the Fens. At its best – and there have been some notable failures – the work is animated by an absorbed interest in ordinary life, in people at the margins of the news, not the charismatic leaders, the intellectuals, the stars. Cromwell appears in *Light Shining in Buckinghamshire* but Mao is absent from *Fanshen*. A democratic company, the plays are infused with a democratic spirit. Typically, Joint Stock shows explore a particular community, caught at a moment of disturbance or adjustment, and we are led to consider a collective destiny, the shifting energies of a common life. This is most obviously true of *Fanshen* – an account of the impact of revolution on a Chinese village – but the definition holds good for much of the later work. The Derby Day crowd in *Epsom Downs*, the painters and decorators in *The Ragged Trousered Philanthropists*, the potato pickers in *Fen* – each are approached on their own terms, their rituals of work and leisure carefully observed, their struggle to make a decent life vividly dramatised.

At the same time, Joint Stock's method of work, both in creating the plays and in creating itself as an organisation, has attracted a lot of interest. Not all the attention has been friendly. Accusations of elitism, of writing plays by committee, of perversely pursuing a method for its own sake, have surfaced from time to time in the press and in theatre bars. 'I've *been* to China and it didn't improve my acting', one actor remarked as *Fanshen* slipped into its tenth week of rehearsal. However, the observation that the company's general way of working is as important a development in contemporary theatre as the achievements of individual productions has been widely made. The key question, of course, is the relationship between the two: how the quality of the work is related to the conditions in which it is created. This is not just a matter of warm rehearsal rooms, genial company, chemistry. Such comforts have often proved elusive over the last twelve years, never more desired than when work starts in a gloomy hall with lukewarm radiators, a blocked toilet, a broken phone. There are rooms and halls scattered across London that only actors, pensioners, the karate club and jumble sale browsers ever see. In places such as these Joint Stock have assembled some of their best work and fiddled, in the break, with the central heating. But if the immediate circumstances differ very little from those endured by other theatre groups, the company have fashioned an approach to making plays that breaks with traditional patterns of production, extending the role of actors, writers, directors and technicians in the pursuit of the one goal that every Joint Stock member, on a good day, would agree upon: excellence.

This is hardly a novel objective – it is an achievement the Arts Council earnestly wishes for all its clients – and a commitment to excellence does not explain why writers like David Hare or Howard Brenton should have produced plays so strikingly different from their other work when writing for Joint Stock. But the emphasis on excellence, on aesthetic standards, is important if the impulse behind the creation of the company is to be correctly identified. The prominence of *Fanshen* – the show which above all established Joint Stock's identity – doubtless explains why it has been seen as a political theatre group. Here was a play about revolution, approached with an evident seriousness and played in a disciplined ensemble manner that surely sprung from a shared ideology. Brecht was mentioned by the critics; a degree of humourlessness – a sure sign of political conviction – noted. Moreover, having enacted the turning over to communism of the Chinese peasants, the company promptly applied the process to itself, eventually establishing a collective, abolishing the post of artistic director and subjecting all aspects of the work from get-ins and get-outs to the choice of future productions, to democratic discussion and control. That the Actors Company had set up a similar democracy two years earlier was beside the point. They were doing Chekhov.

To those who subscribe to the notion that everything is political – now proving as disabling a perspective as it was liberating in the sixties – Joint Stock are clearly more political than the Royal Shakespeare Company or the Theatre of Comedy. But attempting to establish the company's political credentials, to identify a programme that makes sense of the choice of plays, the style of production and the audience reached, will not get us very far. These issues have been discussed, often at great length, and many who have worked for the company have argued for a political assessment of its priorities. The evolution of Joint Stock however, has been more marked by a refusal to adopt fixed principles governing the choice of projects than it has by any ambition to reach a shared political view. The point of departure of the company, the challenges it has set itself and the list of its achievements are, in the first instance, best understood in aesthetic terms. Max Stafford-Clark, the company's first and only artistic director, once described Joint Stock as a 'colourless company' in the sense that the group takes on the complexion of the material with which they are working. Had *Fanshen* been a show about the Stock Exchange, it is unlikely that Joint Stock would have evolved in quite the same way (though the name might have stood). The essential elements of the working method, however, would not have been radically affected. From the outset, the consistent aim has been to create conditions in which new work can be produced to the highest artistic standards.

The period in which the company was established is a difficult one to characterise in any general way. Some of the events of 1973/4 may seem familiar a decade or so later – an Ethiopian famine, a royal wedding, a channel tunnel bill, a miners' strike – but the mood of the times was far removed from the present bleak impasse. That miners' strike, the climax to a sustained period of industrial and political militancy, brought down the Heath Government and few were prepared for the steady erosion of possibility that lay ahead. While Thatcher was organising her bid for party leadership, within the milieu of the alternative society it was still possible to read *Oz*, score from your local dealer, be hassled by the fuzz and consider not working a different condition to being unemployed. But only just. The hedonism of the late sixties had been tempered by a recognition that 'doing whatever the fuck you want' involved a lot of hard work, at least on a long term basis, and, more important, it left the capitalist state intact. It also gave private enterprise – particularly the fashion, music and publishing industries – some highly profitable marketing ideas, which was not quite what had been intended. 1974, the year of Joint Stock's inaugural production, brought one major confrontation between students and the state – the Red Lion Square demonstration – and the Windsor Free Festival attempted to recapture the spirit of the great Hyde Park concerts. But the alliance of rock music and Trotskyism, lifestyle politics and community action had already fragmented. Some had been recruited into the ranks of the revolutionary left; others had settled for hi-fi and *Zen and the Art of Motorcycle Maintenance*; many were talking seriously about careers.

As for the theatre, the underground had become the fringe, the shift in terms fixing a growing sense of remoteness that within the more politicised sectors had led to the formation of groups like 7:84 and now hastened the emergence of others with equally specific programmes. The Women's Theatre Group and Gay Sweatshop both began in 1974. A related desire to address a broader audience prompted writers like Griffiths, Edgar and Brenton to seek production in mainstream theatres. It was no longer enough to talk to sixteen students in a basement, especially the same sixteen every time. The desire to create plays that tackled large public themes required physical and financial resources beyond the reach of the average fringe outfit. Inevitably, this perspective was viewed with suspicion by those who continued to operate out of the back of a Bedford van. There was much talk of opportunism and sell-out. The move was also viewed with suspicion by the managements of mainstream theatres. Brenton's *Measure for Measure*, directed by Bill Gaskill, made it to the main stage in Exeter in 1972 but the theatre's artistic director, Jane Howell, soon packed her bags when the board refused to back her policies. The same year, a touring production of *England's Ireland*, a twelve-actor show with a weekly wage bill of £600, was offered to 54 theatres by an offshoot of Portable Theatre set up by David Hare. Three took up the offer and the company folded. Griffiths' *The Party* and Brenton and Hare's *Brassneck* held main stages in 1973 but Brenton's *Magnificence*, directed by Stafford-Clark, had a rough ride at the Royal Court where some, according to Hare, thought Brenton should be taken out and buried alive in a hole in a field. If fringe theatre was being bought out by the establishment, as some feared, early trading was cautious and highly selective. In any event, many fringe groups were breaking up, if only temporarily – Freehold, Pip Simmons and Portable were among those that ground to a halt in 1973. Exhausted, demoralised, or simply broke, the prospect of doing the same gigs to the same small audiences induced inertia and not a little dismay. The party – or the revolution, depending on how you looked at it – was over.

This barely amounts to a crisis by today's standards. It was still possible to form a company without a preliminary lunch with Mobil Oil or Manpower Services; it was to be some years before the Arts Council began to shoot from the hip and blow its feet off; and if the spectacular growth of the fringe had been checked there were still signs of continuing vitality. Yet there was a definite air of pessimism about future prospects. Bill Gaskill struck a characteristic note in 1973, following his departure from the Royal Court as artistic director. Comparing theatre in Germany with the set-up in England, he concluded that a large, democratic ensemble company of the kind found in most German cities had proved an elusive ideal in England. At the National, star casting and glossy programme notes were more evident than a critical approach to the classics; at the Royal Court, assembling each production on an *ad hoc* basis with a minimum of rehearsal limited the scope for artistic development. Gaskill's repertory experiment at the Royal Court, together with the workshop activities he encouraged, had been attempts to build an informal company of actors equipped with the skills and techniques needed to present difficult and demanding new plays. His productions – particularly the Bond plays and the controversial *Macbeth* – had effected a major change in styles of acting and design. Spare, exact, contemptuous of scenic embellishment and emotional display, they were influenced by the work of the Berliner Ensemble but achieved without the long rehearsal and permanent nucleus of artists available there. Then as now, work was constantly interrupted by the need to turn to the business of producing a commercial success in order to finance the experimental work. In 1973, as now, that meant stars, bright lights, music.

Gaskill was to pursue his vision of an ensemble group with Joint Stock. Fresh from running the Court, he had little desire to join a new company. The impetus to set one up came from the graduates of the fringe, many of whom were equally frustrated with the conditions of their work. Max Stafford-Clark, whose work Gaskill had imported to the Theatre Upstairs, had been artistic director of the Traverse Theatre in Edinburgh from 1966 to 1970, directing plays by a range of new writers including Stanley Eveling and David Mowat, and taking the company from its original home in a former brothel to its present premises. In 1968, inspired by the work of the American troupe Café La Mama, Stafford-Clark set up a permanent company of six actors who spent time between shows in workshop sessions, developing skills and exploring new ways of presenting material. Much of this work was concerned with breaking down the conventional actor/audience relationship, a preoccupation of the period that saw hippy shake hands with hippy, often gave the audience the right to interrupt the action – and the actors the right to blame the audience – and at the extremes led to the gropings, the punch-ups, the vomiting and screaming that made going to the theatre in the sixties such a good night out. The Traverse experiments were comparatively restrained, though writhing on the floor to loud rock music was not unknown and one show was devised that required an audience of one (it sold out). These workshops led to the formation of the Traverse Workshop Company, a group whose methods were to shape the early work of Joint Stock, both in the assumption made that actors could play many parts in the course of the evening – including swapping the same part from scene to scene – and in the role the actors took in generating material for the show through improvisation and research. Among the group were Tony Rohr, Carole Hayman, Toby Salaman and Linda Goddard – who became part of the pool of Joint Stock actors – and in shows like Brenton's *Hitler Dances* and John Spurling's *In the Heart of the British Museum* a new way of working with writers was developed that built on the experiment of earlier multi-authored group shows like *Dracula* – the gory precursor of Portable Theatre's equally gory *Lay-by*.

The Traverse Workshop broke up in 1972, like other fringe groups drained of energy by a spartan existence that for all its excesses – most of which took place in Amsterdam – left much to be desired. Money, warmth and a comfortable van were high on everyone's list and not easily found in Edinburgh. The legacy of the group, fused with Gaskill's work at the Court, was to provide the artistic foundations of Joint Stock. The move to establish the new company, however, was purely practical. Beyond the Court, the Hampstead Theatre Club and the Open Space, London offered no medium-sized space where work of any scale could be attempted. Stafford-Clark's experience at the Court, particularly the battles over *Magnificence*, made it clear that the opportunities in Sloane Square were limited. What was needed was a company that could act as a bridgehead between the small scale studios of the fringe and the bigger stages, a company that could retain the flexible methods of the fringe yet have access to better facilities, reach a broader audience and achieve higher standards.

The vision was shared by many, of course, but it was Stafford-Clark, David Aukin and David Hare who took the initiative in the summer of 1973 and set about creating such a company. Aukin had managed Freehold, organised the Fringe Festival at the Cockpit in 1971 and had a flair for setting up new companies – he had recently formed Foco Novo with Roland Rees. At first, however, it seemed easier to revitalise Portable Theatre. Portable had an established reputation for presenting new work; with Aukin and Stafford-Clark drafted onto the board, the company could claim to be entering a new phase of development. The snag was that Portable had debts, not least with their accountant, and, in a series of exchanges with the Arts Council, it became clear the Council's enthusiasm for the new recruits was as much to do with their potential as guarantors for a bank loan as it was with their professional credentials. Portable, in other words, was not to be baled out. Indeed, later that year, the company that often seemed to have a bizarre fixation with the English police force found itself in court.

In the circumstances, it seemed prudent to create an entirely new company. A policy document was drafted, a name invented – several names in fact, though United Friendly was the only one to make it onto paper before Stafford-Clark came up with Joint Stock. With bankruptcy in the air the former may have had the reassuring ring of a high street building society but the latter more effectively encapsulated the ambition to act as a platform for those with a common interest in new work. Joint Stock was to be an outlet for those who had served an arduous apprenticeship on the fringe. Nancy

Meckler, Chris Parr, Pip Simmons were all mentioned as interested parties and a list of plays by Eveling, Mowat and Snoo Wilson drawn up. The Arts Council liked the idea and offered a grant of £12,000 – a sum in line with Portable's level of subsidy. The money, however, was not to materialise until the spring of 1974, by which time Joint Stock had already toured its first production. To everyone's surprise, it was not one of the scripted plays. It was a production of a documentary novel, used as the basis for an informal actors' workshop organised by Gaskill and Stafford-Clark: Heathcote Williams's *The Speakers*. In the best traditions of the fringe, the workshop was unpaid and had no precise objective beyond allowing Gaskill and Stafford-Clark the chance to see each other work with actors drawn, in the main, from the Traverse group and the Court. For the actors, some of the work was familiar enough – two hours of PT before looking at a text was standard at the time. But being despatched from the rehearsal room to beg on the streets of London during an IRA bomb campaign was a fresh challenge. Tony Rohr, who played McGuinness in the show, was rumbled by an Irish priest: Paul Kember made a fortune. In the event, begging proved to be a useful skill to develop. While DALTA – the Arts Council Touring wing – subsidised a tour of *The Speakers*, a London run at the ICA was only made possible by hustling money from private backers.

Although the success of *The Speakers* made another similar venture a priority, the first full season of work (1974/5) consisted mainly of scripted plays. Stanley Eveling's *Shivvers*, Barry Reckord's *X* and Colin Bennett's *Fourth Day Like Four Long Months of Absence* were all plays commissioned or originally offered productions by other companies. *Shivvers*, written for the Traverse, continued the long partnership between Eveling and Stafford-Clark and was a Joint Stock production in name only, the funds being supplied by the Traverse and the Royal Court Theatre Upstairs. Similarly, *X* had been scheduled for production Upstairs but abandoned for casting reasons; and *Fourth Day* had been considered by Portable and the Oval but dropped for legal reasons – Tom Stoppard was referred to as a sugar plum fairy in one of the tamer passages. Both scripts were now picked up by Stafford-Clark and presented as co-productions with the Theatre Upstairs. Although these plays have since been eclipsed by later Joint Stock work, they did much to consolidate the reputation of the new company. *Fourth Day*, a bizarre picaresque in the tradition of Heathcote Williams's *AC/DC* and Ken Campbell's *The Great Caper*, had a central character who layed into everybody with the relentless intensity of Jimmy Porter on acid, the Actors Company's much publicised venture into democracy, for example, being dismissed as 'a sell-out by a bunch of chocolate-box mother-fukkas.' Its roots, in other words, were in the sixties though, like flares and Greek restaurants, it flourished well enough in the seventies. *Shivvers* and *X*, in their different ways, shared a preoccupation with sex that in retrospect looks like a foundation course for the sticky realism of *A Thought In Three Parts*. Clothes were shed, limbs dusted with baby powder, a parson lounged in bed with a whore. *X*'s full frontal dramatics certainly earned it an enthusiastic reception and the show was given a second late-night run. All three productions were prepared in the conventional way with three or four weeks rehearsal; all three were also directed by the same director, a fact which prompted one or two to ask at an early board meeting if Joint Stock's role as an umbrella company was to do more than keep Max Stafford-Clark out of the rain. A fourth show, *The Doomduckers Ball*, provided the answer. Based on an idea by Neil Johnstone – a Freehold actor – this energetic cabaret about life's losers sported a memorable monologue about Snow White and the seven dwarfs (up at dawn, a ten mile hike to the mines and when they came home they were *still* singing). Hastily assembled, the show emerged from a short workshop to pack the Theatre Upstairs and exhaust the remainder of Joint Stock's first grant.

The major event of 1974, however, was the *Fanshen* workshop. It was not the exhilarating experience *The Speakers* had been. Progress was slow, the subject seemed impossibly remote and there was real confusion and disagreement about what the objectives were. Success tends to glamourise hard work. In retrospect, a morning spent hawking and spitting like Chinese peasants can seem part of a necessary process of evolving a style. It can even sound like good fun. At the time, it seemed pointless, a blundering effort to find a way through a chaos of possibilities. Hinton's book is over 600 pages long. At the end of five weeks, few were convinced there was a play in it. Gaskill's idea to set up the workshop as an exercise in democracy, however, began a process of self-enquiry that was to be decisive in the years ahead. In studying the social existence of the Chinese peasants, the group equipped themselves the better to understand their own. Actors directed, directors acted, all were entitled to question and criticise; pockets were emptied, earnings revealed, status and authority broken down and analysed. All this may not have yielded a play but it presented a challenge. The Long Bow villagers had improved their existence. Joint Stock would do the same.

Seven months later, *Fanshen* opened in Sheffield. The success of the production, however, coincided with depressing news from the Arts Council. An application for £21,000 was met with an award of £14,400. It was an increase but not enough to support the wage rise the company were now determined to implement. Worse, it threatened the plan to install workshops as the basis for future shows. The group was incensed. A campaign was hastily organised, MPs canvassed, Arts Council delegates lobbied. Nothing came of it. Joint Stock refused to compromise, insisted that the quality of their work depended on workshops and cut their programme. As a result, the second season consisted of one show (*Fanshen*) which played for a total of 14 weeks – only three more than it took to prepare. Set against the first year – five shows over 27 weeks for less money – it looked like the surest way to lose a revenue grant. Remarkably, when the company presented an unreformed budget for 1976/77, they won their case. The Council granted a 300% increase (£40,000) with the proviso that shows played for at least as long as they rehearsed. There are few opportunities to feel nostalgic about the Arts Council. This is one of them. From unpaid acting classes, a partnership between two directors and a group of actors had evolved that was to create a new approach to making plays. *Fanshen* exemplified the virtues and the Arts Council responded. Joint Stock began to develop its method. They even got a new van.

The elements of the approach that grew from these beginnings are easily summarised. The essence is the insistence that good work requires time and a nucleus of people who are committed to the matter in hand. Again, commitment here should not be confused with a disposition to change the world. An actor with three lines and an evening of scene shifting may feel inclined to change the world but is better placed to take it out on the furniture – watch the stage being cleared at a matinée in the Olivier. Joint Stock's approach simply puts the actors' energy to better use, securing a commitment to the work by maximising the involvement of each. Eventually, this was to extend to running the company but initially it was more a matter of enriching the actors' work in rehearsal. An extended preparation period, typically ten weeks, is divided into a four week workshop and a six week rehearsal. During the workshop, actors, writer and director explore the subject matter, each contributing ideas and undertaking research. Improvisation, talks by experts (anything from 'The causes of the First World War' to 'The life of an English bookie'), interviews with character models, research trips, reading sessions, group discussions, a vast assortment of games and exercises (for analytical purposes more than diversion), crash courses in professional skills – all are used to generate material for the play. In the second stage of the process – the gap between workshop and rehearsal – the writer composes the play. This is not, as is sometimes assumed, a question of scripting improvisations or following instructions drawn up by the group. The writer's work remains an independent creative act and the result may have no obvious relationship to the material yielded by the workshop: the *Fanshen* workshop did not produce the theme or narrative of the play, though it taught David Hare a great deal about Chinese prostitutes, peasant eating habits, and the dramatic interest of dialectical debate; the *Cloud Nine* workshop never ventured into Victorian Africa. One of the many new experiences the process affords the writer is confronting a group of actors who know a great deal about the subject of the play. Allied with the actors' expectation that the piece will offer them the chance to show their skills across a range of parts or within a single substantial role – and this is the logical outcome of the whole approach – the gathering of the group for the final stage of the process – the rehearsal – can be terrifying. It is certainly never dull.

In practice, there has been considerable variety in the way this basic structure has been used. In some cases, the point of departure for the workshop has been a book, either to be dramatised (*Speakers, Fanshen, Philanthropists, Harlots High and Low*) or to serve as an introduction to a subject (Mary Chamberlain's *Fen Women* for *Fen*, Wesley's work for *Say Your Prayers*). Often, a project has started with the actors undertaking research on a community visited or lived in during the workshop (*Borderline, Fen, Celestial Cow, Standing Corn, Fire in the Lake, Deadlines*) or alternatively with the actors researching their own social experience (*Cloud Nine, Optimistic Thrust, Real Time*). Again, workshops have started with a script already drafted (*Devil's Island, Epsom Downs*) or with just a dramatic model in mind (*Mad World*). On three occasions (*Yesterday's News, Optimistic Thrust, Real Time*), they have been set up or completed without a writer and the material has been improvised by the actors, though the results – writers will be pleased to note – have been generally considered less successful. More usually, preparation for the workshop involves much discussion between writer and director as possible themes and approaches are refined (*Light Shining* began with the Crusades; *Cloud Nine* was planned as a show about emigrants to America) and only once has the subject changed completely during the course of the actual workshop (*Yesterday's News*).

Whatever the original idea, the constant feature – and the attraction of the method – is the opportunity to devise a programme of work appropriate to the subject. Over the years, Joint Stock actors have found themselves at race meetings and picket lines, in sleazy massage parlours and cramped country cottages; they have become skilful decorators, expert con-artists and diligent reporters; met peers, politicians, soldiers, villains, farmers, nurses, preachers, labourers – the list is not endless but the contrast with a cup of tea, a read through of a script and on with the blocking could not be more emphatic.

During the first phase of the company's work – from *The Speakers* to the break up of the permanent company in 1977 – the workshop method evolved in a gradual way. Ideas were questioned, problems identified, solutions tried out. One early problem was ensuring the actors from the workshop would be available for the final production. Both *The Speakers* and *Fanshen* had gone into rehearsal with several actors new to the project. For *Yesterday's News*, the first show of 1976, Gaskill suggested a continuous ten-week period without a writing gap. The idea was to draw on the actors' own sense of community, using personal histories as a point of departure then moving out to do research in Camden Town. Jeremy Seabrook was invited to write the play. After several weeks, work ground to a halt. If *Fanshen* had consciously set out to break down traditional writer-director-actor roles, it happened spontaneously on *Yesterday's News*. Gaskill lay on the floor and laughed in what looked like an admission of defeat. It was. The initiative was taken up by the actors, David Rintoul suggesting a story about the massacre of British mercenaries in Angola (the Colonel Callan affair) that had appeared in the morning paper. Paul Kember, an ex-journalist, contrived an interview with the recruiting agent and, together with Philip McGough, taped a conversation in the Tower Hotel. When the company heard the tape – it was an interview all Fleet Street had been trying to secure – they decided to follow it up. A journalist, a stockbroker with African investments, a survivor of the expedition, a girlfriend and two mercenaries were added to the mix of stories gathered by the group and brought back to the workshop.

Yesterday's News produced several new developments. Unlike the previous shows, the actors were responsible for finding characters and recreating them in the workshop. As directors, Gaskill and Stafford-Clark had no privileged knowledge of the material they presented. More important, the company as a whole had to frame a point of view of what was a shocking and controversial story. After *Fanshen* it might be thought a revolutionary perspective was adopted. Far from it. The politics were largely determined by the accidents of the research. Indeed, three of the actors left the workshop, uneasy about the project. Pauline Melville thought a play about Angola that gave no voice to an African or Cuban soldier would be politically incoherent and merely glamorise the British mercenaries. There is little doubt that in production the soldiers were the most compelling characters on stage. The stark simplicity of the staging – the characters talking to the audience, as to an interviewer, sitting in chairs – provided the perfect stillness to heighten the violence of the content. Artistically, it was a model of realistic acting – cool, detailed, the energy contained but pressing on the surface. Stafford-Clark was to use the same format for the second act of *Falkland Sound*, in name a Theatre Upstairs production but in spirit a Joint Stock show. Again, a stockbroker, a girlfriend, a journalist were among the voices used to dimension the central experience of a serviceman who, in this case, had not survived the Falklands War.

The inclusion of a journalist in these shows is revealing. The figure represents the outsider's point of view and tends to be invested with the anxieties the director and actors feel about their responsibility to the people whose lives they are 'reporting'. The difficulty of arriving at a political perspective within the group is then directly dramatised in the character of the journalist. The device was used again in *Borderline*, Hanif Kureishi's study of Asian immigrants in Southall, also directed by Stafford-Clark. It is a common enough device, but no substitute for the debate that would be available if all the parties to a political conflict were represented. In *Borderline* the absent voice was the white racist, excluded initially because it was felt it was a known position. But when the decision was taken to allow two white actors to play Asians – essentially to keep the group together and protect aesthetic standards – the absence of that voice jeopardised the political argument of the play. The conflict within the journalist between a fuller political commitment and the pressures to succeed at her job took on an added, and not wholly unintended, resonance.

In any actual situation, problems of this kind are not easily solved. Accidents and chance encounters are an inherent part of the workshop process. Time and again, characters, situations, fragments of action are discovered in unexpected ways. The entrance of the mercenaries in *Yesterday's News*, for example, was based on the moment the real mercenaries burst into the rehearsal room and swiftly checked the exits before talking to the group. Clearly, the journey of a workshop is often richer and more rewarding when there is a general sense of direction but no specific destination in mind, no prepared argument or point of view. Not the least of the challenges a writer takes on when working with Joint Stock is the task of persuading the group to accept the view taken of a subject that has been collectively examined. But there is always a risk the work will move into territory where, in the time available, the group is ill-equipped to deal with the discoveries made. Consensus breaks down, people leave, practical considerations – getting the show on – assume priority. There was no Angolan in *Yesterday's News* because there was none to be met. Fabricating an African character would not have answered the problem. Set against the detailed realism of the other figures it would have been shallow and unconvincing. If it is too simple to say the aesthetics determined the politics – in practice it is never as clear-cut – it is nevertheless in the interplay of the two that any real analysis has to begin.

A second problem that arose as the workshop method was embraced was organising the programme of productions. With the expansion of the output in 1976/77 it made financial sense to try and overlap the work and use the same pool of actors. Already there were discussions about forming a permanent company and finding a London base. The issues were taken up at board meetings. The company had initially been set up with a board of directors (Aukin, Hare and Stafford-Clark were joined by Gaskill and the designer Hayden Griffin in 1974). As the administrative work increased, a general manager, Graham Cowley, was appointed. Actors had attended these meetings from the outset. In the wake of the *Fanshen* workshop, their representation was formalised, resolutions were passed making minutes and budgets available to all and equal wages was confirmed as company policy. The style of the meetings changed, influenced by the manner of the Long Bow villagers. Carole Hayman's début as a minute-taker, for example, was pronounced a failure when she recorded personal remarks. At Hare's insistence, the minutes were redrafted and lively exchanges ('Are we just a company that does books or what?'; 'Oh do shut up. The very word "spies" freezes my piss') were toned down for posterity. Inevitably, perhaps, there was a demand for more meetings as the actors were anxious to keep in touch with future plans and exert an influence on the choice of projects. Early policy statements had asserted the plays would be chosen by the directors 'with the help of the actors'. Now a proposal to give the actors first refusal on future projects was debated. Gaskill and Stafford-Clark rejected the idea, arguing that subject matter had an influence on casting and that recruiting new actors was an added stimulation to the work. As ever, the first priority was to create the best conditions to serve the work and fixed rules were viewed with some scepticism.

As work progressed, however, there was a growing feeling that the company had become too disparate. Scheduling three shows for 1976/77, so that the actors from *The Speakers* and *Fanshen* could do all three, proved impossible. After *Yesterday's News*, two separate groups were formed: one to work with Stafford-Clark and Caryl Churchill on *Light Shining*, the other with Hare and Tony Bicât on *Devil's Island*. When a surplus in the budget made an extra scripted play possible – Wallace Shawn's *A Thought in Three Parts* – a third group was assembled. The season was – and so far remains – Joint Stock's most productive. *The Speakers* was revived, just made it to the Belgrade Festival – the van broke down in Munich – and went on to cause a riot in Dublin. In all, the total number of weeks performed reached 42, 26 in London and 16 on tour. When the plans for 1977/78 were drawn up, however, it was decided to concentrate resources and attempt a continuous period of work with a single group of actors. A permanent company was formed, the Roundhouse offered a London base for the season and, in the Theatre Upstairs at the end of 1976, Joint Stock decided to become a collective.

The one exception to the resolution, naturally enough, was the artistic director. Stafford-Clark was reluctant to give the actors the right to veto future projects, especially as there was no guarantee they would stay together beyond the year. (They didn't.) With the programme for the year already decided – two workshops shows, *A Mad World My Masters* by Barrie Keeffe and Howard Brenton's *Epsom Downs* were to open the Roundhouse season – Stafford Clark's reservations had little immediate application, but they served to highlight the underlying issue: was Joint Stock to be a fully democratic body in which the majority ruled or, in the final analysis, was authority to rest with the directors? In other words, what was Joint Stock? The ensuing discussions were often intense, rarely dull and offered many different answers. Gaskill's vision of the company was of an ensemble group with a specific approach to its craft. Operating as a collective had an obvious practical value but the superior goal was fashioning a common method of work. For Gaskill, *Fanshen* had been the decisive breakthrough in this respect and it remained the measure by which he judged subsequent Joint Stock productions. The dialectical techniques used in the *Fanshen* rehearsals to break down the content of each scene had been refined into a sophisticated critical tool. Stafford-Clark, as he recalls it, 'discovered Brecht'. Ultimately, the approach supposes a political point of view – what the action is intended to show has to be decided in political rather than psychological terms – and certain aesthetic preferences come into play: the emotional temperature is muted, the stage cleared of distractions, the acting honed to essentials. Gaskill saw the collective as an opportunity to take this work a stage further, the company's own practice mirroring the struggle to achieve a shared perspective in the work.

For Stafford-Clark, on the other hand, what defined Joint Stock was less a particular approach, more a commitment to general excellence. Essentially a pragmatic view, it entailed no less exacting demands but it stressed the need to remain flexible, altering methods and techniques to suit the material in hand. Among the actors, Paul Freeman shared this emphasis on excellence, Simon Callow (much to his own surprise) initially supported Gaskill, though the alliance did not last long. The debates continued throughout the year, carefully recorded by Stafford-Clark in a succession of notebooks. But it was the work itself that threw the issues into relief. Securing an extra two weeks' rehearsal, Gaskill applied the *Fanshen* methods to Barrie Keeffe's spirited comedy. The work was hard, detailed and relentless: eleven days were spent on the first scene, devising slogans to fix the political argument, questioning every line, stripping the text bare. By the time the show opened, the actors were exhausted and Callow called for a post-mortem on the rehearsals, seeing in Gaskill's increasingly autocratic manner a denial of the collective philosophy of the group: 'Democracy exists at meetings but it's back to the Middle Ages for rehearsal.' Whatever Joint Stock was, it was not there to allow directors to shout at actors.

In *Being An Actor*, Callow describes this episode to illustrate how the original Joint Stock collective, whatever the democratic pretensions, remained firmly ruled by the tastes and disciplines of its directors. By coincidence, *Mad World* started rehearsal the same week the Berlin Schaubühne arrived in London with their celebrated production of *Summerfolk*, directed by Peter Stein. A collective of thirty, with a subsidy of £1.5 million, the virtues of the production were perceived to rest upon a two-month rehearsal period, extensive research and Peter Stein's habit of working with the same nucleus of actors. The ideals of the two companies were broadly the same and, unknown to each other, the actors shared a common frustration. Unlike Joint Stock, the Schaubühne actors had the right to veto the choice of plays, each project being put to a vote. But despite the formal safeguard against the breakdown of consensus, they revealed during the course of their visit that once work started things were a little different: Peter Stein tended to be an autocrat in rehearsals.

It is hard to imagine a collective directorship working in practice, easy to see how compromising a director's contol can dilute the results. Joint Stock have never embarked on the experiment, though the actors have been drawn into ways of working that are far removed from orthodox practice. During *Mad World* rehearsals, a day was spent discussing casting, each actor explaining the combination of parts they found most challenging. If the final decisions left some more content than others – Gillian Barge did not relish the part of Vi but finished up playing it – it was, as Bob Hamilton observed, a measure of the actors' involvement that the question of what stimulated their energies was opened up at all. Again, the idea for the character of Gran and several key script developments came from the actors. The post-mortem on rehearsals produced no clear consensus about actor–director relationships. Will Knightley felt Joint Stock's approach was too cerebral; Tony Rohr wanted more individual attention; David Rintoul believed writers were nurtured at the expense of the actors; Paul Freeman thought Callow confused the idea of the collective with the integrity of the individual functions within it. If Joint Stock has worked best when there has been a strong team of directors – and this is what the evidence suggests – that is not to excuse pettiness and abuse from directors, nor is it to deny the talent and enterprise of the actors. Problems inevitably arise when agreement breaks down, both in rehearsal and committee. Tears are shed, tempers frayed, egos crushed. The first Joint Stock collective had its fair share of bitter wrangles and the directors did not always come out on top. During the preparations for *Epsom Downs*, Stafford-Clark's authority was directly challenged by the actors. Unconvinced the play would work in the Roundhouse – a converted engine shed with a cavernous acoustic – he tried to persuade the group to switch venues. The actors were against it and so was Howard Brenton – 'If I can't fill 400 seats I'd rather blow up and rot in a debtors' gaol'. Stafford-Clark refused to compromise. Finally, Paul Freeman forced the issue and proposed that either Stafford-Clark direct the show at the Roundhouse or the collective hire another director. Stafford-Clark went to the Roundhouse.

Whatever the rows and disputes, the collective running of the company released an energy and commitment from all that made the season happen. There were plenty of problems to tackle. The Arts Council grant of £50,000 was £27,000 short of what had been budgeted to finance the programme. Negotiations with the Roundhouse broke down when the administration changed hands and *Mad World* had to move to the Young Vic. The scale of the shows made finding touring venues equipped to take them difficult (only *Mad World* toured). These issues were threaded through the weekly meetings of the collective, discussed alongside company wages (raised from £50 to £65), writers' contracts, publicity, a party for the Roundhouse staff, foyer exhibitions, stage management requirements, travel arrangements. More important, both *Mad World* and *Epsom Downs* had an enthusiastic reception. However arduous the process, the work was exceptional: cripsly performed, visually striking and – no bad thing – hugely entertaining. London audiences reached 20,000, almost double the previous year's figure and a massive improvement on the first season (1,000). If Joint Stock's audience was more likely to fill the Young Vic than the Roundhouse, the challenge of expanding the scale of the work and pitching at a broader audience had been met. Touring, for practical reasons, was cut back and only a revival of *Fanshen* brought the total up to ten weeks. It was the obvious show to revive and it marked the end of the first phase of the company's life. As the money ran out, enthusiasms ebbed and the group began to disperse. The *Guardian* ran a story on the arts page: 'Britain's first and last entirely democratic theatre company . . . going out of business' – the Actors Company had run out of ideas and decided to break up. Joint Stock's 'temporary closure' was reported further down the column. The Actors Company has never resurfaced. Joint Stock did.

The departure of the original group of actors and the increasing involvement of Gaskill and Stafford-Clark in work outside the company, however, meant there was some slackening of energy and momentum. There is a moment in the life of most theatre groups when the peeling away of the personalities who built them threatens to leave an artistic vacuum. The office, the van, the policy papers remain, but as succeeding directors take on the inheritance and try to shape it to fresh purpose the real power passes into the hands of the administrators. In the eighties, this has become a very common trend. The Arts Council now demands a degree of administrative stamina and ingenuity from its clients that leaves little reserves for art. It is to Joint Stock's credit that they have resisted this pressure, though the group's recent history reflects the bureaucratic character of the times. Company minutes for 1977 weighed in at 14oz, excluding agendas; by 1984, with less work in production, they had broken the 3 lb. barrier, despite a flirtation with cheaper paper. Committees have flourished, the first emerging after the permanent company disbanded. The Joint Stock Non-Employed Provisional Policy Steering Committee, as Graham Cowley christened it, was charged with the task of heaving the group back into life. Significantly, it was Stafford-Clark who took the initiative in setting up a co-production with the Royal Court of Snoo Wilson's *The Glad Hand*. There was some concern among the committee about resuming production with a scripted play, and an attempt was made to ensure Joint Stock actors formed a majority of the cast. In the event, only two of the old collective took part and the production was seen by critics and audiences alike as a Royal Court venture – a problem of identity that was to recur when Stafford-Clark became artistic director of the Court in 1979. However, two workshop shows were eventually chosen for 1978. Gaskill assembled a new team of actors to work with Stephen Lowe on *The Ragged Trousered Philanthropists* and Stafford-Clark and Caryl Churchill worked with a second group on *Cloud Nine*. If the previous season ended with doubts about the future, 1978 produced an effective and potent regrouping. At first, it seemed the new nucleus of actors might provide the basis for a continuous cycle of work. Plans were laid to mount a production of a classic in the gap between the *Philanthropists* workshop and rehearsals but were finally scrapped as it would have meant a new Joint Stock company appearing in their first show without the benefit of a workshop on the script. Instead, the actors organised their own project – *Next*, from a script by Sean McCarthy – and presented it at the Oval.

    With two separate acting groups, familiar problems reappeared, 'What is Joint Stock?' being among them. In principle, it was agreed that each company should operate as a collective, controlling its own budget and sending two delegates to the steering committee to co-ordinate future plans. In practice, this meant one group taking decisions that affected the other. When the *Philanthropists* sanctioned an overspend on their show, the money, in effect, had to be taken from the *Cloud Nine* budget. This prompted some to suggest that the general manager assume overall responsibility for financial affairs but the move was resisted by Gaskill. The actors' awareness of the conditions of their work had been the logic at the heart of Joint Stock's development, their involvement in the running of the company the key to its success. Graham Cowley was spared the role of company dictator and a new wave of Joint Stock actors were forced to admit they could count.

    There was, however, a more fundamental problem. When Gaskill was appointed associate director at the National and Stafford-Clark took up a similar position at the Royal Court, it was clear Joint Stock would not travel the route of the original collective and form a permanent ensemble (Gaskill, in fact, took the *Philanthropists* actors with him). Early in 1979, a subcommittee was set up to recruit a new director and Richard Wilson was invited to direct a workshop show. Wilson had worked at the Stables Theatre Club in Manchester in the early seventies and gone on to establish a varied career as a stage and television actor. With Joint Stock, he had, to say the least, a hard act to follow. With the exception of *Devil's Island*, Gaskill and Stafford-Clark had directed all the company's major shows. If they had every reason to wish Wilson success, there were nevertheless doubts about a new director and actors matching the quality of the past work. Joint Stock had evolved a distinct style, even if the collaboration of Gaskill and Stafford-Clark had been thought to preclude the possibility of one emerging. With *The House*, David Halliwell's delicate study of class tensions in a First World War hospital, Wilson and his team pulled it off. The production was in the best traditions of Joint Stock's work – high grade ensemble playing, a fastidious attention to detail and a clarity of purpose in both writing and directing. Whatever the change in accent and personality, the ingredients of the Joint Stock method remained a fruitful mix in different hands.

The subcommittee that appointed Wilson continued to meet during the preparations for *The House* and it became the basis for a new Policy Committee, the body that remains the artistic executive of the company. Among its first decisions, was the abolition of the post of artistic director. There was no palace revolution, no knives were flourished, no backs stabbed (the chief back was not at the meeting). It was merely a recognition that, with Stafford-Clark poised to take over the Royal Court, direction of the company had effectively passed into the hands of the new committee. The committee consisted of representatives from past shows and *The House* company, a combination of old hands and new faces that was to be formalised as the constitution of Joint Stock. A brief constitutional crisis had arisen earlier when the *House* company, sensitive to the drudgery involved in running institutions like hospitals or touring theatre groups, generously awarded the general manager a pay rise. In the transition to the new constitution it was unclear whether they had the authority to do this. (Had *The Philanthropists* followed their earlier instincts, the general manager could probably have done it himself.) An AGM of all Joint Stock members – those who had worked for the company since it began – was convened in the summer to finally sort out who was in charge and subject the Policy Committee to democratic election. The important feature of the arrangement was the weight given to those actually creating the work. This is the cornerstone of Joint Stock's philosophy and it was one of four principles laid down as central to the company's future operations. The others restated lessons learned: equal pay for all, productions to play for as long as they rehearsed and touring to equal the length of the London run. Over the next two years, the arrangements were refined as the company assumed its present form: a shifting collective, each group handing on responsibility to its successors, with experienced members in place to ease the transition.

The unknown factor was whether artistic growth could be achieved where there was no guaranteed continuity of personnel. After *The House*, Gaskill returned, his residency at the National proving short-lived, and the question was temporarily deferred. At first, Gaskill planned a production of *Timon of Athens*, a project he had earlier suggested to Hare and Bicât. However, as it offered no opportunity for actor research and had no need of a writer it was dropped in favour of *An Optimistic Thrust*. Although a writer was initially involved, this became a wholly improvised show, continuing Gaskill's long fascination with mask work. It was, by all accounts, a remarkable workshop but the experiment failed to carry through into performance. As Joint Stock turned the corner into the eighties, it had for the first time gathered a comprehensive set of bad notices. On tour, the actors arrived at one venue to find the poster amended by a nervous management to read '*An Optimistic Thrust* – Starring Julie Covington'. It was a denial of everything Joint Stock stood for and a sign of changing times.

The first two seasons of the eighties were more variable in quality and less certain in direction than at any time in the past. The growth in subsidy that allowed the output and the scale of the work to expand in the seventies came to an end. The Arts Council continued to hand out money (£64,000 in 1979/80 rose to £73,000 the following year) but there was increasing talk of empty pockets, difficult days, honest work to be done in the regions. (As if to prove the point, the Council started to take its money back – along with everyone else, Joint Stock had to return 1% of its grant in 1983). From 1979, the output settled at two shows a year, offering between 18 and 22 weeks of performances, sufficient to make an impact but not enough to conceal failure. As the gap between shows lengthened, many people began to wonder if Joint Stock still existed. After *Real Time* opened in January 1982, a whole year passed, the Falklands crisis came and went (Gaskill dropped a Green Peace project as the flag-waving began) before a new show finally appeared. Within the company, 'What is Joint Stock?' became a matter of some urgency but the topic was increasingly 'postponed to the next meeting'. David Hare wrote to say all things come to an end and this was probably it, a proposal that was as unwelcome as it was pertinent.

Elsewhere, 'What is Joint Stock?' was getting more immediate attention. The Arts Council threatened to demote the company to special project status, an administrative realm from which there is no return. The two successes of the period – a revival of *Cloud Nine* and Hanif Kureishi's *Borderline* – were both co-productions with the Royal Court, initiated by Stafford-Clark. If Joint Stock had once been 'the Royal Court in exile', as Edward Bond had put it, it now looked as if the Royal Court had come home, taking Joint Stock with it. The company's independent ventures beyond Sloane Square seemed hesitant and unconvincing. Wilson's second workshop show – Nick Darke's *Say Your Prayers* – was disappointing, the character of the Frog a twee invention set against the horses in *Epsom Downs*, however expertly performed. Unusually, the workshop spent little time researching material for the play – a risk that did not pay off. Jack Shepherd's improvised piece, *Real Time*, equally failed to translate the excitement of the workshop to the stage, a problem that recalled the mistakes of *An Optimistic Thrust* and suggested lessons had not been learned. After a ten week workshop, there was still no play and the show opened disastrously in Plymouth. People began to leave at the interval.

Solutions to these problems were not easily found, though they were eagerly sought as new recruits took over the company. As always, the recipe for past success looked infuriatingly simple. In 1973, Stafford-Clark and Gaskill had chatted on the steps of the Court, set up an informal workshop and *The Speakers* had appeared. They had had no resources beyond an enthusiasm for the idea. In the eighties, however, no one would do unpaid work, especially for Joint Stock. A plan for a series of exploratory workshops came to nothing, the energy diverted into unsuccessful applications for funds. The company had a grant of £73,00 but it also had an obligation to produce shows. Spontaneity gave way to more cautious deliberation. David Rintoul argued for a return to a permanent company; Gaskill proposed an actors' laboratory based around the *Optimistic Thrust* group; Stafford-Clark offered to host a director's workshop at the Court, but the spark needed to reignite the passions of the group failed to catch.

The Policy Committee created a Projects Committee to review applications for workshop shows, for with few proposals emerging from inside the group, ideas had to be imported and Joint Stock began to resemble the production facility that had been the inspiration of its founders. New actors brought fresh minds to policy discussions as the *Prayers* company handed on to *Borderline* and they, in turn, to *Real Time*. But they also brought a comparative lack of experience in instigating work. Unlike other groups, Joint Stock commits to a play in advance of reading a script. Assessment is speculative, guided by instinct and a sense of past form. It is also more crucial: a four week workshop on an indifferent project is a miserable, dispiriting experience. There are few occasions in Joint Stock's life when an idea has been met with instant and enthusiastic support. Stafford-Clark's Crusades project only interested two of the *Yesterday's News* actors; Hare and Bicât's proposal for *Devil's Island* was initially coolly received. What made the shows happen was their directors' determination to weather the long faces, the yawns, the shrugs. That directorial function was now generalised throughout the committee structure of the group and it took some time to recover the confidence and daring needed to push projects through. This remains a problem with Joint Stock, though it is not necessarily an argument for an artistic director. Recently, a move was made to invite Gaskill to assume overall direction – since 1979 he has only returned to direct one show – but nothing came of it. The solution lay elsewhere. After an uncertain two years, a new generation of directors began to voice their passions and obsessions within the group.

With Caryl Churchill's *Fen*, Joint Stock emerged from what begins to look like a transitional phase in its development. In a sense, the success of the show had been prepared for. The director, Les Waters, served his apprenticeship with Stafford-Clark at the Court. He assisted on the original production of *Cloud Nine* (sharing a train with an American baseball team to give notes in Stirling), co-directed the revival and had initiated a working relationship with Caryl Churchill by the time they embarked on *Fen*. Extra funds were secured from Eastern Arts to allow the company to spend two weeks living in the Fens; the designer, Annie Smart, took part in the workshop – the Policy Committee subsequently made provision for designers in workshop budgets routine – and a haunting set was devised that allowed the play's twenty-one scenes to move with the minimum of interruption. For the first time, the Almeida Theatre, still in the process of refurbishment, hosted the London run. Bare walls, freezing temperatures and a mist that slowly engulfed the auditorium were conditions that would not have suited many plays – *A Thought in Three Parts* would have been unthinkable – but they were splendidly apt for *Fen*. At the press night, there were screams – not at the axe murder (two gasps, one 'Oh my god') but at the appearance of the victim's ghost seconds after the body had been locked in a wardrobe. It was, in all senses, a chilling evening.

Fen was an unexpected success. Rather as the *Fanshen* company had imagined little interest beyond the ranks of the Anglo-Chinese Friendly Society, so the *Fen* actors thought the desolate lives of a group of rural women would make for problems at the box office. *Fanshen* celebrated change; *Fen* fixed an experience of broken hopes and mute despair. Yet, the show successfully transferred to the Public Theatre in New York and was remounted with an American cast when the original production returned to London for an additional run at the Court. As it was the first Joint Stock production for nearly a year, there was an obvious need to mount a second. The Arts Council had become a regular and intrigued correspondent: where was the £83,000 grant for 1982/3? In the absence of a workshop project, Howard Barker's *Victory* was entrusted to another Royal Court graduate, Danny Boyle. There was the usual anxiety about presenting a scripted play and some resistance to elements of the Joint Stock approach among the cast – not every actor finds the induction into collective working inspiring. For a new director, a Joint Stock show is always a daunting prospect. Boyle had the added pressure of knowing the production was destined for the main stage at the Court, a space where failure is all too conspicuous and usually met with a polite suggestion that the culprit try a few classics in the regions. In the event, *Victory* proved Barker's most popular play of the period and Boyle, despite stomach cramps and a colourful array of cold sores, was allowed back into his office.

Fen and *Victory* were quickly followed by Nicholas Wright's adaption of Balzac, *The Crimes of Vautrin*. Gaskill had convened the workshop in the autumn of 1982 but rehearsals did not commence until the spring of 1983. This meant Joint Stock had three productions opening in the space of six months, much to the relief of the Arts Council and the evident satisfaction of the Policy Committee. The Council allowed expenditure on *Fen* to be rolled forward into the new financial year and awarded a grant of £89,000 for 1983/4 – a 7½% increase. The busy schedule was largely unintended, the result of a long fallow period in 1982, and it posed a few problems. One consequence of the extended gap between the *Vautrin* workshop and rehearsals was the loss of four of the actors from the original workshop. Together with the technical complexity of the show, this entailed additional rehearsal on the road. Touring all three shows continued to offer its peculiar blend of misery and elation. The *Victory* stage management only coped with the Glasgow to London leg of the tour by taking a generous view of the provisions of the Road Traffic Act. As a result, a committee was set up to monitor stage management affairs and ensure touring schedules drew on the expertise of stage managers past and present. (A touring company needs to keep its drivers in one piece.) Both the *Victory* and *Fen* actors returned from the regions delighted on the whole with the reception of the work but dismayed by the suspension in the minibus. Not for the first time, a resolution was passed condemning minibuses in general and RBF 413T in particular. Earlier, the *Fen* actors, unaware of the ovation that awaited them in New

York (and the less welcome attentions in the city's subway – Waters met more baseball players) had arrived at the University of East Anglia to find few students, fewer posters and little interest in the show. Publicity was discussed and students categorised with minibuses: slow, unreliable and boring. Meanwhile, the Sherman Theatre wrote to complain about the *Victory* and *Vautrin* posters – 'hideous' was the implication of the message from Cardiff – and in Glasgow there were grumbles about Balzac going on for two-and-a-half hours without due warning. Little did they know it was a miracle *Vautrin* went on at all. Preparations for the show had been unexpectedly disrupted in the first week of rehearsal when Chris Fulford was struck by lightning and fell through a shattered manhole cover. He rejoined the cast after what was euphemistically described as 'a well-earned rest'. As with *Victory*, the scale of *Vautrin* involved the stage management in a work load described by the actors as 'staggering'. The Policy Committee, now well into its stride and heartened by the success of the work, broke with convention and paid the hard-pressed crew above the company wage. The principle of equal pay was breached, though the extra was reckoned at the rate of the additional stage manager the crew must have dreamed of and divided equally among the team.

Securing touring venues suited to each production is always a problem for Joint Stock. Often, dates are booked in advance of any precise technical information about the show. *The Great Celestial Cow*, Sue Townsend's festive account of Asian women in Leicester – the second production of 1983/4 – played a combination of small community venues as well as Leicester Haymarket and the main stage at the Court. If the facilities to present the play were more readily available in Leicester and London, the substance of the piece made Bradford an obvious port of call. In principle, Joint Stock shows are geared to meet the demands of the London venue – a bias common to other touring groups – and adapted as best they can to smaller spaces. In this case, 'as best they can' meant the lighting board nearly blew up in Edinburgh while in Sheffield such hazards were not even on the agenda – there were no lights. The director, Carole Hayman, was the first woman to tackle a Joint Stock show – ten years after *The Speakers*, *Celestial Cow* was in fact the anniversary production – and she celebrated the event by restaging twenty-five scenes in a fetching twilight in Yorkshire. Sue Townsend took the unusual step of rewriting her contract to share her royalties with the actors, a decision which prompted the Policy Committee to examine the whole question of writers' contracts and Joint Stock's participation in the profits from the plays. Writers are the only people to be issued with a formal contract by the company, just as they alone are paid during the gap. If the contribution of actors and directors to the final text is sometimes the subject of after-hours debate ('The bike wasn't *his* idea, you know') it has so far resisted exact contractual definition. Like 'What is Joint Stock?' and 'The Gap', 'Royalties' is an item certain to be tabled for discussion as long as Joint Stock survives.

Fresh impetus for the future came with a series of short, exploratory workshops held in the summer of 1984. The idea had been suggested by Gaskill as a way of testing potential projects and allowing new members to take on workshop work without the pressure of a final production. In all, four workshops took place, each involving some actors from past shows. The subjects ranged through immigrant labour, male attitudes to women, television news and the miners' strike, and although each workshop was limited to a week, the exercise proved productive. Carole Hayman's group spent three days in Barnsley with the Woman Against Pit Closures organisation, visited the picket lines and still found time to take in the TUC conference in Brighton. Simon Curtis – Royal Court trainee – led a raid on Fleet Street, coaxed a few journalists to tell the truth and spent a few hours in the ITN newsroom ('It's all lies,' was the early verdict). These two projects were taken up and went into production in 1985, *Amidst the Standing Corn* in a co-production with the Soho Poly, *Deadlines*, after a further workshop, with the Theatre Upstairs. While they were in preparation, Gaskill agreed to share the honours on a Howard Barker script with Kenny Ireland, one of the *Philanthropists* actors. Scheduling problems, however, meant Ireland had to face *The Power of the Dog* alone and so become the seventh different director in succession to mount a Joint Stock production.

Co-productions look set to remain the only method of sustaining the present level of output, though a proposal to effect a permanent arrangement with the Royal Court was rejected by the Policy Committee, ever anxious to avoid restricting the work to one kind of theatrical space. The most recent show at the time of writing, Karim Alrawi's *Fire in the Lake*, was presented in association with the Liverpool Playhouse and is the only Joint Stock show never to be seen in London. A change of director between workshop and rehearsals, together with the loss of several actors, left the writer with conditions of work he could easily have found elsewhere. Following hard upon the discovery that 'administrative incompetence' and 'collective naïvety' had allowed a deficit of £60,000 to accumulate, Joint Stock almost succeeded in providing a sensational conclusion to the present account of their history. For those who recalled Portable's run-in with the law over National Insurance, the revelation of a similar debt twelve years later had an ominous ring.

Happily, the crisis was weathered, the deficit paid off and production resumed. That it did is largely due to the commitment of a new generation of actors and directors who have recognised the unique possibilities a company like Joint Stock affords for experimental work. The future will very much depend on the drive and ambition of directors. For, with the exception of Caryl Churchill, there has never been a prolonged relationship between the company and particular writers. For some, perhaps, the pressures of the workshop, the obligation to write under the constant gaze of the actors, is too public an exposure of a craft more easily controlled in private. Certainly, for an inexperienced writer, the process is exacting, with little room for manoeuvre as rehearsal draws nearer. ('I like the first act' can be a very unnerving compliment.) The Company's latest project, *A Mouthful of Birds*, will be the first show to be written by two writers – Caryl Churchill and David Lan – and the workshop includes a choreographer and dancers – evidence of a continuing effort to experiment with fresh combinations of skills in creating the work. Such departures are not without their hazards. Les Waters' introduction to dance work earned him two cracked ribs and a punctured lung, not the ideal condition in which to direct a show.

The future will also depend on the actors, not just as managers of the company's affairs. From the outset, Joint Stock's work has been noted for the quality of the acting. In the first place, this is made possible by long, concentrated rehearsal. Often in the three-week scramble to get a show on, actors can come to see their characters as less complex than themselves. An attitude or a feeling is seized on – this man is arrogant, clever, this woman is sad, neurotic – and what we get in performance is an exaggeration, an intensification of a partial truth, played for all it is worth. The arrogant man shouts, the sad woman mopes and we become restless and bored even though we are watching *Hamlet*. The manner is plain in what is usually dismissed as rep acting – a style directly related to its conditions of production, though by no means exclusive to regional reps. A quick turn around of shows – *Hay Fever* one week, *Mother Courage* the next – means that conventions of movement and speech are simply rearranged to suit, as best they can, the broad outlines of the part. Wit in a dressing-gown gives way to gravity in a boiler suit. Talent and technique can work wonders in three weeks but desperate notes from a harassed director, already casting *Me and My Girl*, are never far away: 'Please try and be better' is often all, in the time available, that can be said.

The Joint Stock process allows the actors to develop a more complex view of their characters. Where the workshop explores lives that are incorporated into the final play, the actors bring to the rehearsal text a rich supply of observations that enable the characters to be more densely realised. To live in the Fens, for example, and work on the land provides an opportunity to absorb a sense of a place and its people that has an obvious practical value: tones of voice, styles of behaviour, patterns of work and recreation can be tested against what is known or assumed in advance about the community. It is important not to idealise this process: it usually begins with awkward, comical encounters between self-conscious actors and bemused or suspicious locals – 'I'm with Joint Stock Theatre Group' can prove as arresting an opener as double-glazing or Jehovah on the doorstep; it can proceed in a random, superficial way that would appal any self-respecting historian or sociologist; and the results may be nothing more than vague impressions, a collection of puzzling details. The benefit of the research is that it complicates received ideas about the subject. To an outsider – even the most observant actor – a day's labour in a muddy field, a glimpse of a cheerless kitchen, an evening listening to gossip in a bar may at first only confirm expectations about the people who live this life. The monotony of the work, the isolation, the drabness of the streets suggest a simple attitude to its limitations. Then, as the work progresses, as people begin to talk and tell stories, the generalisation breaks down and much more contradictory impulses and feelings are caught. To see these contradictions, to recognise the conflicting tensions within an individual life, is to restore a complexity to character work that, in practice, is so often denied in the name of consistency.

It is, of course, the writer's task to make sense of the lives encountered in this way. But the initial workshop is always group work and what typically evolves is a sense of responsibility to the people whose experience is to be dramatised. In some cases, as in *Cloud Nine*, the experience is the actors' own personal lives and the writer is then under pressure to give back to the actors a play that does justice to the intimate feelings and anxieties revealed in the workshop. Again, actors may challenge the writer's vision of a world that has been collectively examined, as happened on *Epsom Downs*. But it is the constant effort to be truthful to the people who are to be presented that characterises the workshop and carries forward into rehearsal. To see people in their fullness and individuality, to recognise what is particular to each, becomes an obligation to portray their lives with an exactness that neither parodies not patronises their experience. It is a humanist impulse and one that tends to characterise any group work that begins in an exploratory way, driven by a passion for human detail, for scraps of real life, rather than a predetermined ideology. The self-discovery of the group, the space given to each member to share their ideas and feelings, fosters an open, critical attitude that brings with it the pleasures of learning and the labour of understanding. Choices have to be made: which people? what do we say about them? The following pages record some of the answers.

PART TWO

PRODUCTIONS:

AN ILLUSTRATED CHRONOLOGY

Previous page: the first workshop for *The Speakers*; Bill Gaskill (left)
and Max Stafford-Clark. (Photographer unknown.)
Above: Heathcote Williams (*left*) watching Tony Rohr.

The Speakers
adapted by William Gaskill and Max Stafford-Clark from the book by Heathcote Williams

Workshop group
Alan Armstrong, Kenneth Cranham, Leonard Fenton, Paul Freeman,
Robert Hamilton, Mona Hammond, Carole Hayman, Annie Holloway,
Pauline Kelly, Paul Kember, Pamela Moisewitsch, Peter Postlethwaite,
Chris Ravenscroft, Struan Rodger, Tony Rohr, Toby Salaman

Cast

Oliver Cotton	AXEL NEY HOCH
Paul Freeman	JACOBUS VAN DYN
Roderic Leigh	SOCIALIST SPEAKER/NORMAN/NEWS VENDOR/COLIN/BOLLING/NAB OFFICER/ MARY PICKFORD/POLICEMAN
Roger Lloyd Pack	HARRY/POLICEMAN/DOCTOR/DAVIES/ PRISON WARDER/DEALER
Tony Rohr	WILLIAM MACGUINNESS
Struan Rodger	CAFFERTY
Toby Salaman	LOMAS
Jennie Stoller	FREDDIE KILLENEN/GLADYS/BETTY DRACUP/SINGING WOMAN/ROWTON HOUSE CLERK
Directed by	William Gaskill and Max Stafford-Clark
Designed by	Miki van Zwanenberg
Stage Manager	Ross Murray
Lighting by	White Light
Produced by	David Aukin

First performance: Birmingham Repertory Studio, 28 January 1974
Subsequently: ICA, 30 April 1974, with Cecily Hobbs and Kenneth Cranham
replacing Jennie Stoller and Struan Rodger

Left to right:
Deirdre Costello, Bill Stewart and Tony Hagarth.
(Photo: Nobby Clark.)

Shivvers
by Stanley Eveling
A co-production with the Traverse Theatre and the Theatre Upstairs

Cast

Tony Hagarth	WALTER
Bill Stewart	VIC
Deirdre Costello	MAUREEN
Directed by	Max Stafford-Clark
Designed by	Poppy Mitchell

First performance: Traverse Theatre Club, Edinburgh, 12 April 1974
Subsequently: Theatre Upstairs, Royal Court, London, 14 May 1974

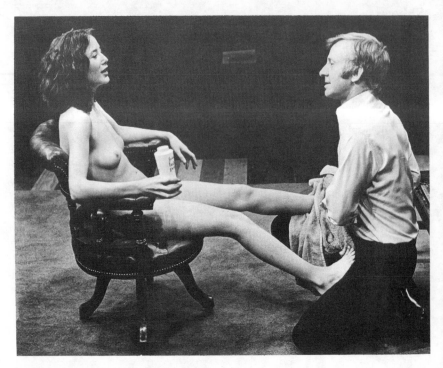

Libba Davies and Terence Frisby.

X
by Barry Reckord
A co-production with the Theatre Upstairs

Cast

Terence Frisby	FATHER
Libba Davies	NANCY
Margaret Burnett	WARDRESS/CROWN/DEACONESS
Roderic Leigh	JUDGE/PRESSMAN
Directed by	Max Stafford-Clark
Designed by	Douglas Heap

First performance: Theatre Upstairs, Royal Court, London, 12 August 1974

Tony Rohr. (Photo: Joe McKeever.)

Fourth Day Like Four Long Months of Absence
by Colin Bennett
A co-production with the Theatre Upstairs

Cast

Carole Hayman	GIRL/MELITA/MRS SIMPSON
William Hoyland	JIM/BILL/SAM/DETECTIVE
Caroline Hutchinson	JANE/DORIS/NANCY
Malcolm Ingram	PROFESSOR SAMSON/CLIVE/MR ROACH/ DOCTOR
Tony Rohr	CHELSEA CHAMBERS
Toby Salaman	SID/MR PARSONS/SIR GEORGE LOCKSPUR

Directed by	Max Stafford-Clark
Designed by	Diana Greenwood
Lighting by	White Light
Stage Manager	Ross Murray
General Manager	Graham Cowley

First performance: Traverse Theatre Club, Edinburgh, 15 October 1974
Subsequently: Theatre Upstairs, Royal Court, London, 5 November 1974

Carole Hayman (*left*) and Dinah Stabb.
(Photo: Gerald Murray.)

The Doomduckers Ball
by the Company, based on an idea by Neil Johnston

The Company
Carole Hayman
Mary Maddox
Dinah Stabb
Jeff Teare

The Band
Dave Brown
Boot Cartwright
Lyn Edwards
Rob Pope

Choreography by	Sue Lefton with John Amiel
General Manager	Graham Cowley
Stage Director	Nicky Crosby
Stage Manager	Rick Shannin
Road Manager	Rodger Needham
PA	Roy Trueman

First performance: Oval House, London, 6 March 1975
Subsequently: Theatre Upstairs, Royal Court, London, 25 March 1975

Left to right: Philip McGough, Pauline Melville, Paul Freeman, Tony Mathews, Tony Rohr, Roderic Leigh, David Rintoul and Cecily Hobbs.

Fanshen
by David Hare, based on the book by William Hinton

Workshop group
Oliver Cotton, Kenneth Cranham, Marty Cruickshank, Paul Freeman,
William Gaskill, David Hare, Carole Hayman, Cecily Hobbs, Roderic Leigh,
Roger Lloyd Pack, Pauline Melville, Toby Salaman, Max Stafford-Clark

Cast

Philip Donaghy	CHENG-KUAN/SECRETARY LIU/TAO-YUAN
Paul Freeman	T'IEN-MING/CHANG-CHUER/HUAN-CHAO
Cecily Hobbs	HSUEH-CHEN/OLD LADY WANG/HSIEN-E
Roderic Leigh	FA-LIANG/LITTLE LI
Philip McGough	TUI-CHIN/SECRETARY CH'EN/TING-FU
Tony Mathews	KUO-TE-YU/SHEN CHING-HO/HOU PAO-PEI
Pauline Melville	CHUNG LAI'S WIFE/CHI-YUN/SHENG CHING-HO'S DAUGHTER
David Rintoul	MAU-HSI/WEN-TE/CHUNG-WANG/LAI-TZU
Tony Rohr	YU-LAI/YUAN-LUNG

Directed by	William Gaskill and Max Stafford-Clark
Designed by	Di Seymour
Lighting by	White Light
Stage Manager	Bess Manning
Costumes made by	Andrea Montag
General Manager	Graham Cowley

First performance: Crucible Studio Theatre, Sheffield, 10 March 1975
Subsequently: ICA Theatre, London, 21 April 1975

The production was remounted at the Hampstead Theatre Club with Marty
Cruickshank, Paul Kember, Will Knightly and Toby Salaman replacing
Pauline Melville, David Rintoul, Roderic Leigh, and Philip Donaghy.

First performance: 14 August 1975

David Rintoul (*left*) and Paul Kember.
(Photographer unknown.)

Yesterday's News
by the Company and Jeremy Seabrook

Workshop group
Gillian Barge, William Gaskill, Linda Goddard, Cecily Hobbs, Paul Kember,
Pauline Melville, Will Knightley, Tony Mathews, Philip McGough,
David Rintoul, Jeremy Seabrook, Max Stafford-Clark

Cast

Gillian Barge	JOURNALIST
Linda Goddard	GIRL
Paul Kember	TONY
Will Knightley	JONES
Tony Mathews	STOCKBROKER
Philip McGough	ROCHE
David Rintoul	MICK

Directed by	William Gaskill and Max Stafford-Clark
Designed by	Hayden Griffin
Lighting by	Rory Dempster

First performance: West End Centre, Aldershot, 6 April 1976
Subsequently: Theatre Upstairs, Royal Court, London, 11 May 1976

Left to right: Nigel Terry, Linda Goddard,
Will Knightley, Carole Hayman and Colin McCormack.

Light Shining in Buckinghamshire
by Caryl Churchill

Workshop Group
Colin Bennett, Ian Charleson, Caryl Churchill, Jenny Cryst, Linda Goddard,
Carole Hayman, Will Knightley, Colin McCormack, Anne Raitt,
David Rintoul, Max Stafford-Clark

Cast

Jan Chappell*	BROTHERTON/HOSKINS/FIRST WOMAN/ WILDMAN
Linda Goddard	HOSKINS/WIFE/SECOND WOMAN/RICH/ BROTHERTON
Robert Hamilton	SERVANT/STAR/MAN/SEXBY/BUTCHER/ DRUNK
Will Knightley	BRIGGS/CLAXTON/IRETON/VICAR
Colin McCormack	VICAR/FRIEND/STAR/COBBE/CROMWELL/ BRIGGS
Nigel Terry	COBBE/BRIGGS/PREACHER/ RAINBOROUGH/STAR

Directed by	Max Stafford-Clark
Designed by	Sue Plummer
Stage Manager	Alison Ritchie
Costumes made by	Linda Hemming and Sue Thompson
Lighting designed by	Steve Whitson
Musical Director	Colin Sell
General Manager	Graham Cowley

First performance: Traverse Theatre, Edinburgh, 7 September 1976
Subsequently: Theatre Upstairs, Royal Court, London, 21 September 1976

* when indisposed replaced by Carole Hayman

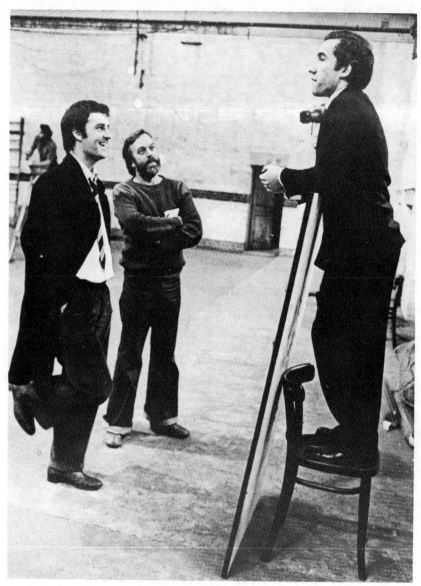

Left to right: Paul Kember, Bill Gaskill and Simon Callow.

The Speakers

adapted by William Gaskill and Max Stafford-Clark from the book by Heathcote Williams (Revival)

This revival played at the Bitef Festival, Belgrade, Hamburg and the Dublin Theatre Festival before touring Britain.

Cast

Simon Callow	SOCIALIST SPEAKER/NORMAN/NEWS VENDOR/COLIN/BOLLING/NAB OFFICER/ MARY PICKFORD/POLICEMAN
Philip Donaghy	LOMAS
Cecily Hobbs	FREDDIE KILLENEN/GLADYS/BETTY DRACUP/SINGING WOMAN/ROWTON HOUSE CLERK
Paul Kember	CAFFERTY
Tony Mathews	AXEL NEY HOCH
Philip McGough	JACOBUS VAN DYN
David Rintoul	HARRY/POLICEMAN/DOCTOR/DAVIES/ PRISON WARDER/DEALER
Tony Rohr	WILLIAM MACGUINNESS

Directed by	William Gaskill and Max Stafford-Clark
Designed by	Miki van Zwanenberg
Lighting by	Nick Heppell
Stage Manager	Abigail McKern
General Manager	Graham Cowley

First London performance: Conway Hall, 20 October 1976

Left to right: Jane Wood, Simon Callow,
Gillian Barge, David Rintoul and Suzanne Bertish.

Devil's Island
by Tony Bicât

Workshop group
As production except Philip Donaghy replaced Tom Wilkinson

Cast

Gillian Barge	BETTY
Suzanne Bertish	JILL
Simon Callow	KUTCHEVSKI
Philip Donaghy	HUGH
David Rintoul	BILL
Jane Wood	SUE

Directed by	David Hare
Designed by	Hayden Griffin
Lighting by	Rory Dempster
Stage Manager	Alison Ritchie
Assistant Stage Managers	John Morton, Alastair Palmer
Hair by	Carol and Robin of the Ginger Group
General Manager	Graham Cowley

First performance: Sherman Theatre, Cardiff, 11 January 1977
Subsequently: Royal Court Theatre, London, 23 February 1977

Robyn Goodman.

A Thought in Three Parts
by Wallace Shawn

Cast
Summer Evening
Philip Sayer	DAVID
Robyn Goodman	SARAH

Youth Hostel
Jack Klaff	DICK
Stephanie Fayerman	HELEN
Robyn Goodman	JUDY
Paul-John Geoffrey	BOB
Philip Sayer	TOM

Mr Frivilous
Tony Rohr	MR FRIVILOUS

Directed by	Max Stafford-Clark
Designed by	Sue Plummer
Lighting by	Steve Whitson
Stage Manager	Abigail McKern
Assistant Stage Manager	Martin Hutchings
Set built by	Philip Parsons
General Manager	Graham Cowley

First performance: ICA, London, 21 February 1977

Left to right: David Rintoul, Gillian Barge,
Robert Hamilton and Will Knightley.

A Mad World, My Masters
by Barrie Keeffe

Workshop group
As production

Cast

Gillian Barge	VI SPRIGHTLY
Simon Callow	RONALD SAYERS
Paul Freeman	MR ROBERTSON/CHARLIE
Robert Hamilton	BILL SPRIGHTLY
Cecily Hobbs	JANET CLAUGHTON
Will Knightley	MR FOX
David Rintoul	HORACE CLAUGHTON
Tony Rohr	DOCTOR O'FLAHERTY/GUARD
Jane Wood	GRANDMA SPRIGHTLY/ELIZABETH

Directed by	William Gaskill and Max Stafford-Clark
Designed by	Hayden Griffin
Company and Stage Manager	Alison Ritchie
Deputy Stage Manager	Donna Rolfe
Assistant Stage Manager	Alastair Palmer
General Manager	Graham Cowley

First performance: Young Vic Theatre, London, 28 April 1977
The production was remounted at the Roundhouse as part of the Joint Stock season; first performance: 7 September 1977

Will Knightley riding Tony Rohr.

Epsom Downs
by Howard Brenton

Workshop group
As production

Cast

Gillian Barge	SHARON/MISS MOTROM/WOMAN IN BEER TENT	Will Knightley	MR TILLOTSON/ HUGH/JOCKEY/ POLICEMAN/ KERMIT FROG TRADER
Simon Callow	SANDY/THE AGA KHAN/LES BACKSHAKER/ BEER TENT DRUNK/ HORSE OWNER	David Rintoul	BOBBY/POLICE HORSE/JOCKS/THE AGA KHAN'S BODYGUARD/ JUBILEE CHICKEN TRADER/THE DERBY
Paul Freeman	LORD RACK/ RODGER COYLE/ JUBILEE DRUNK/ STABLE LAD/ SAWBONES, A HORSE/BUD	Tony Rohr	CHARLES PEARCE/ MACK/MORRY/A HORSE RUNNING IN THE DERBY/THE COURSE
Robert Hamilton	SUPERINTENDENT BLUE/MAN DOWN ON HIS LUCK/ GRANDPA/LOUIS/ BEER TENT DRUNK/ HORSE OWNER	Jane Wood	PRIMROSE/EMILY DAVISON/DOROTHY DELAUNE/CYNTHIA BACKSHAKER
Cecily Hobbs	MARGARET/MINTY/ BUNNY GIRL/ HORSE OWNER		

The company also plays: Lester Piggott's Fans; Tick Tack Men; Bookmakers; Jockeys; Crowds; Drunks; Lovers and Asylum Inmates.

Directed by	Max Stafford-Clark
Designed by	Peter Hartwell
Lighting by	Gareth Jones
Sound by	Bill Cadman
Company and Stage Manager	Alison Ritchie
Deputy Stage Manager	Donna Rolfe
Assistant Stage Manager	Alastair Palmer
Publicity	Sue Hyman
New auditorium designed by	Hayden Griffin
General Manager	Graham Cowley
Production Manager	Jon Cadbury

First performance: The Roundhouse, London, 4 August 1977

Left to right: Gillian Barge, Paul Freeman, Will Knightley, Robert Hamilton, Bruce Alexander, David Rintoul and Tony Rohr.

Left to right: Simon Callow, Paul Freeman, Bruce Alexander, Will Knightley, David Rintoul and Robert Hamilton

Fanshen
by David Hare, based on the book by William Hinton (Revival)

Cast

Bruce Alexander	YU-LAI/YUAN-LUNG
Gillian Barge	HSUEH-CHEN/OLD LADY WANG/ HSIEN-E
Simon Callow	FA-LAING/LITTLE LI
Paul Freeman	TUI-CHIN/SECRETARY CH'EN/ TING-FU
Robert Hamilton	KUO-TE-YU/SHEN CHING-HO/HOU PAO-PEI
Cecily Hobbs	CHUNG-LAI'S WIFE/CHI-YUN/ SHEN CHING-HO'S DAUGHTER/ HSIN-AI
Will Knightley	MAU-HSI/WEN-TE/CHUNG-WANG/ LAI-TZU
David Rintoul	T'IEN-MING/CHANG-CHUER/ HUAN-CHAO
Tony Rohr	CHENG-KUAN/SECRETARY LIU/ TAO-YUAN

Directed by	William Gaskill and Max Stafford-Clark
Designed by	Di Seymour
Lighting by	Rory Dempster
Company and Stage Manager	Alison Ritchie
Deputy Stage Manager	Alastair Palmer
Production Electrician	Martin Aubrey
General Manager	Graham Cowley

First performance: University of East Anglia, Norwich, 29 September 1977
Subsequently: Oval House, London, 5 October 1977

Left to right: Antony Sher, Nicholas le Provost,
Will Knightley, Olivier Pierre and Thomas Baptiste.

The Glad Hand
by Snoo Wilson
A co-production with the Royal Court Theatre

Cast

Thomas Baptiste	UMBERTO
Rachel Bell	KATHLEEN HOOLEY
Alan Devlin	BRIAN HOOLEY
Julian Hough	CARSON
Will Knightley	WISHBONE
Nicholas le Provost	MARKS
Di Patrick	SYLVIA
Olivier Pierre	LAZARUS
Manning Redwood	CLEMENTS
Tony Rohr	BILL HOOLEY
Antony Sher	RITSAAT
Gwyneth Strong	WILLYA
Julie Walters	MARILYN

Directed by	Max Stafford-Clark
Assistant Director	Les Waters
Designer	Peter Hartwell
Lighting	Jack Raby
Sound	John Delnero
Stage Manager	Alison Ritchie
Deputy Stage Manager	Mark Ashley
Assistant Stage Manager	Tim Welsh

First performance: Royal Court Theatre, London, 11 May 1978

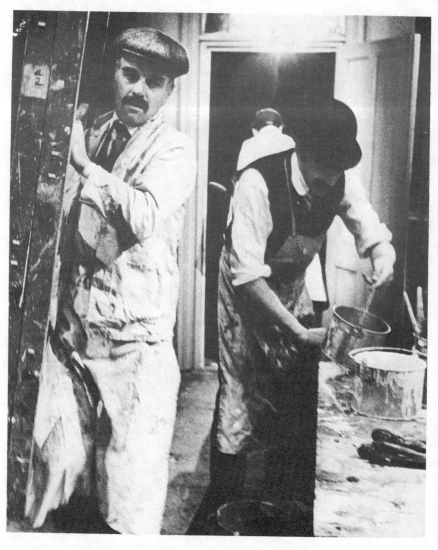

Fred Pearson (*left*) and Peter-Hugo Daly.

The Ragged Trousered Philanthropists
by Stephen Lowe, based on the book by Robert Tressell

Workshop group
As production except Fred Pearson replaced Peter Jonfield

Cast

Bruce Alexander	EASTON/LINDEN/GRINDER
Christian Burgess	SAWKINS/MAYOR SWEATER
Peter-Hugo Daly	CRASS/REV BELCHER
Kenny Ireland	PHILPOTT/RUSHTON
Fred Pearson	OWEN/DIDLUM
Harriet Walter	BERT/ELSIE/MRS SWEATER
Mark Wing-Davey	HARLOW/LETTUM

All the cast, except Peter-Hugo Daly and Fred Pearson, play Hunter.

Directed by	William Gaskill
Designed by	Peter Hartwell
Lighting by	Andy Phillips
Production Manager	Jon Cadbury
Stage and Company Manager	Alison Ritchie
Lighting operated by	Lolly Schenk
Assistant Stage Manager	Danny Boyle
Artistic Director	Max Stafford-Clark
General Manager	Graham Cowley

First performance: Plymouth Arts Centre, 14 September 1978
Subsequently: Riverside Studios, London, 12 October 1978

Next
by Sean McCarthy

Devised and staged by the author with Bruce Alexander, Christian Burgess, Peter-Hugo Daly, Kenny Ireland and Mark Wing-Davey, this production was given three performances at the Oval House, London, on 27-29 July 1978, during the gap between the *Philanthropists* workshop and rehearsals.
It was designed and lit by Peter Hartwell and Lolly Schenk, stage managed by Barry Cunningham.

Left to right:
Antony Sher, Carole Hayman and Julie Covington.

Cloud Nine
by Caryl Churchill

Workshop group
As production plus Dave Hill and Jane Wood

Cast

Act One

Antony Sher	CLIVE
Jim Hooper	BETTY
Tony Rohr	JOSHUA
Julie Covington	EDWARD
Miriam Margolyes	MAUD
Carole Hayman	ELLEN
William Hoyland	HARRY BAGLEY

Act Two

Julie Covington	BETTY
Jim Hooper	EDWARD
Miriam Margolyes	VICTORIA
William Hoyland	MARTIN
Carole Hayman	LIN
Antony Sher	CATHY
Tony Rohr	GERRY

Directed by	Max Stafford-Clark
Designed by	Peter Hartwell
Music by	Andy Roberts
Assistant Director	Les Waters
Lighting Designer	Robin Myerscough-Walker
Costumes made by	Sylvia Kennedy
Production Manager	Jon Cadbury
Company and Stage Manager	Paul Roylance
Assistant Stage Manager	Danny Boyle
Administrator	Graham Cowley

First performance: Dartington College of Arts, Devon, 14 February 1979
Royal Court Theatre, London, 29 March 1979

Left to right: Brian Pettifer, Petra Markham,
Patrick Field, Paul Jesson, Stephen Tiller.
(Photographer unknown.)

The House
by David Halliwell

Workshop group
As production plus Bill Bailey

Cast

Marty Cruickshank	SISTER EUPHEMIA MAXTON
Patrick Field	PRIVATE STANLEY ROBINSON
Paul Jesson	PRIVATE ALBERT JACKSON/CAPTAIN LOCKE
Petra Markham	CYNTHIA BRAITHWAITE
Brian Pettifer	PRIVATE BILLY MEECHAN
Dinah Stabb	JESSICA TOWNSEND
Stephen Tiller	PRIVATE RICHARD PRESLAND

Directed by	Richard Wilson
Designed by	Sue Plummer
Lighting by	Gerry Jenkinson
Assistant Director	Danny Boyle
Production Manager	Jon Cadbury
Stage Manager	Derek Laskie
Deputy Stage Manager	Diana Maxwell
Assistant Stage Manager	Malcolm Heywood
Lighting Operator	Hugh Laver
Administrator	Graham Cowley

First performance: Dartington Hall, Devon, 26 September 1979
Subsequently: ICA, London, 24 October 1979

Left to right: Christian Burgess, Julie Covington, Bruce Alexander, Paul Jesson and Pauline Melville

An Optimistic Thrust
devised and written by the company

Workshop group
As production plus Nigel Baldwin, Philip Davis and Jean Hart

Company
Bruce Alexander
Christian Burgess
Julie Covington
Paul Jesson
Pauline Melville
David Rintoul

Directed by	William Gaskill
Designers: set	Mary Moore
costumes and masks	Jennifer Carey
assisted by	Charlotte Goodfield and
	Catherine Martineau
Lighting by	Steve Whitson
Production Manager	Jon Cadbury
Company and Stage Manager	Alison Ritchie
Deputy Stage Manager	Jamie Rix
Set painted by	James Helps
Music by	Pete Atkin
Administrator	Graham Cowley

First performance: Nuffield Studio Theatre, Lancaster, 20 February 1980
Subsequently: Young Vic Theatre, London, 11 March 1980

Maggie Steed.

Cloud Nine
by Caryl Churchill (Revival)
A co-production with the Royal Court Theatre

Cast

Act One

Graeme Garden	CLIVE
Ron Cook	BETTY
Anthony O'Donnell	JOSHUA
Harriet Walter	EDWARD
Anna Nygh	MAUD
Maggie Steed	ELLEN
Hugh Fraser	HARRY BAGLEY

Act Two

Maggie Steed	BETTY
Graeme Garden	EDWARD
Harriet Walter	VICTORIA
Hugh Fraser	MARTIN
Anna Nygh	LIN
Anthony O'Donnell	CATHY
Ron Cook	GERRY

Directed by	Max Stafford-Clark and Les Waters
Designed by	Peter Hartwell
Music by	Andy Roberts
Lighting Designer	Robin Myerscough-Walker
Stage Manager	Alison Ritchie
Deputy Stage Manager	Julie Davies
Assistant Stage Manager	Malcolm Heywood
Administrator	Graham Cowley

First performance: Royal Court Theatre, London, 1 September 1980

Philip Donaghy. (Photographer unknown.)

Say Your Prayers
by Nick Darke

Workshop group
As production

Cast

Philip Donaghy	PAUL
Judy Elrington	ELMYA
Elizabeth Estensen	NANGOLL
Patrick Field	JOHN WESLEY BENSON
Robert Hickson	REV BRIAN HAYCRAFT/TYCHICUS
Richard Howard	ONESIMUS
Shona Morris	FROG

Directed by	Richard Wilson
Designed by	Peter Hartwell
Lighting Designer	Dick Johnson
Original music by	Andrew Dickson
Movement by	Jo Jelly
Production Manager	Jon Cadbury
Stage Management	Camilla Reeves, Malcolm Heywood, Norma Thompson
Touring Electrician	Hugh Laver
Administrator	Graham Cowley

First performance: College of St Mark and St John, Plymouth,
8 January 1981
Subsequently: Riverside Studios, London, 3 February 1981

Left to right: Lesley Manville, Vincent Ebrahim,
Michael Lightfoot, Deborah Findlay, Rita Wolfe and Nizwar Karanj.

Borderline
by Hanif Kureishi
A co-production between Joint Stock and the Royal Court Theatre

Workshop group
As production

Cast

David Beames	AMJAD/ANWAR/WHITE NEIGHBOUR
Vincent Ebrahim	HAROON/FAROUK/ANIL
Deborah Findlay	BANOO/YASMIN
Nizwar Karanj	RAVI
Michael Lightfoot	BILL
Lesley Manville	SUSAN/VALERIE
Rita Wolf	AMINA

Directed by	Max Stafford-Clark
Designed by	Peter Hartwell
Lighting Designer	Hugh Laver
Production Manager	Jon Cadbury
Stage Management	Michael Lightfoot, Julie Davies
Touring Electrician	Hugh Laver
Assistant Designer	Anabel Temple
Administrator	Lynda Farran
Publicity	Shreela Ghosh

First performance: Jackson's Lane Community Centre, London,
1 October 1981
Subsequently: Royal Court Theatre, London, 2 November 1981

Chas Bryer (*left*) and Anthony Trent.
(Photographer unknown.)

Real Time
collectively written by Chas Bryer, Beverley Foster, Neale Goodrum,
Ingrid Haskal, Derek Laskie, Frances Lowe, Robby Nelson,
Alan Partington, Jack Shepherd, John Tams, Anthony Trent,
Paul Woodrow

Cast

Chas Bryer	BERNARD CUNNINGHAM/WALTER
Beverley Foster	LINDA BAINBRIDGE
Neale Goodrum	RODGER BARNES/ROY GOSLING/KEITH
Frances Lowe	MARY REID/JACKIE PLUMMER
Alan Partington	SANDY CLARKE/ARTHUR BAINBRIDGE
Robby Nelson	HELEN BARNES/ADA MATTHEWS/
	MRS WILLIAMS
Anthony Trent	DAVID KERSHAW

Doctors, Squatters, Travellers, Shoppers played by the company.

Directed by	Jack Shepherd
Designed by	John Halle
Script work by	John Tams
Stage Management	Derek Laskie, Ingrid Haskal
Touring Electrician	Alan Day
Lighting Designer	John Halle
Sound Effects	John Tams
Administrator	Lynda Farran

First performance: College of St Mark and St John, Plymouth,
                            22 January 1982
Subsequently: ICA, London, 23 February 1982

Amelda Brown.

Fen
by Caryl Churchill

Workshop group
As production

Cast

Linda Bassett	SHIRLEY/SHONA/MISS CADE/MARGARET
Amelda Brown	BOY/ANGELA/DEB/MRS FINCH
Cecily Hobbs	JAPANESE BUSINESSMAN/NELL/ MAY/MAVIS
Tricia Kelly	MRS HASSETT/BECKY/ALICE/IVY
Jennie Stoller	VAL/GHOST
Bernard Strother	WILSON/FRANK/MR TEWSON/GEOFFREY

Directed by	Les Waters
Designed by	Annie Smart
Lighting by	Tom Donnellan
Original Music by	Ilona Sekacz
Production Manager	Sheelagh Barnard
Stage Managers	Alan Day, Ingrid Haskal
Costume Supervisor	Marion Weise
Publicist	Eddie Tulasiewicz
Administrator	Lynda Farran
Lighting Assistant	Nick Jones

First performance: University of Essex Theatre, Colchester, 20 January 1983
Subsequently: Almeida Theatre, London, 16 February 1983

Left to right: Julie Covington, Martin Stone, Toby Salaman, Kenny Ireland, Nigel Terry, Hugh Ross, Peter Lovstrom, Adam Robertson and David Lyon.

Victory   *Choices in Reaction*
by Howard Barker

Cast

Julie Covington	BRADSHAW/CLEVELAND
Eleanor David	DEVONSHIRE/CROPPER/GWYNN/ PYLE
Kenny Ireland	BALL/HAMPSHIRE/STREET/ MONCRIEFF
Peter Lovstrom	NODD/SHADE/BEGGAR/FEAK
David Lyon	HAMBRO/GAUKROGER/ FOOTMAN
Adam Robertson	DARLING/PONTING/BANK GUARD/BEGGAR
Hugh Ross	CLEGG/MOBBERLEY/ROAST
Toby Salaman	SCROPE/SOMERSET/UNDY
Martin Stone	McCONOCHIE/BOOT/ SOUTHWARK/PARRY/BEGGAR
Nigel Terry	CHARLES/EDGBASTON/MILTON

Directed by	Danny Boyle
Designed by	Deirdre Clancy
Lighting by	Gareth Jones
Sound by	Patrick Bridgeman
Assistant Director	Simon Curtis
Production Manager	Sheelagh Barnard
Stage Managers	Gill Fox, Richard Oriel
Acting Assistant Stage Manager	Adam Robertson
Wardrobe Supervisor	Pam Tait
Administrator	Lynda Farran
Publicity	Eddie Tulasiewicz

First performance: Gardner Centre, Brighton, 17 February 1983
Subsequently: Royal Court Theatre, London, 23 March 1983

Left to right: Christopher Fulford, Joanne Walley,
Chas Bryer, Fred Pearson and Noreen Kershaw.

The Crimes of Vautrin
by Nicholas Wright after Honoré de Balzac

Workshop group
Oliver Cotton, Christopher Fulford, William Gaskill, Peter Hartwell,
Noreen Kershaw, Patrick Malahide, Tony Rohr, David Stacey, Tusse Silberg,
Leslee Udwin, Nicholas Wright

Cast

Chas Bryer	THE BARON NUCINGEN/M. CAMUSOT/ LE BIFFON
Christopher Fulford	LUCIEN DE RUBEMPRE/LOUCHARD/ CORENTIN/THE DORE CALVI
Noreen Kershaw	MME CAMUS/MME VAL-NOBLE/KATT/ PRUDENCE SERVIEN known as EUROPE/ CHAMBERMAID TO ESTHER VAN GOBSECK
Pauline Melville	LYDIA/JACQUELINE COLLIN known as ASIA/COOK TO ESTHER VAN GOBSECK/ FRANCOISE COUNTESS DE SERISY/ BIBI-LUPIN
Tony Rohr	THE DUKE DE GRANDLIEU/THE ABBE CARLOS HERRERA
Fred Pearson	THE COUNT DE GRANVILLE/ DR DESPLEIN/THE BARON NUCINGEN'S CASHIER/PEYRADE/TOPINARD/99
Joanne Whalley	COQUART/ESTHER VAN GOBSECK

Directed by	William Gaskill
Designed by	Peter Hartwell, Deirdre Clancy
Lighting Designed by	Andy Phillips
Sound by	John Leonard
Assistants to director	Pat and Jude Kelly
Production Manager	Sheelagh Barnard
Costume Supervisor	Nina French
Wardrobe Mistress	Marion Weise
Stage Managers	Sue Darke, Stephen Brady
Touring Electrician	Paul Saunders
Publicist	Eddie Tulasiewicz
General Manager	Anne Louise Wirgman

First performance: Dovecot Arts Centre, Stockton-on-Tees, 12 May 1983
Subsequently: Almeida Theatre, London, 22 June 1983

Left to right: Souad Faress, Lou Wakefield,
Meera Syal, Jamila Massey, Zohra Segal.

The Great Celestial Cow
by Sue Townsend
Presented in association with the Royal Court Theatre

Cast

Bhasker	PRINCESS/MARTIN/HARMONIUM PLAYER/KISHWAR/ASIAN ELDER/ MR PATEL/COW IN FIELD
Souad Faress	SITA
Shreela Ghosh	PRINCESS/RACHEL/LILA/CLASSICAL INDIAN DANCER/INDIRA/RAM/NURSE
Jamila Massey	DAHEBA/STEWARDESS/1ST OFFICIAL/ FAT AUNTIE (MASI)/LIBERAL/SARLA
Dev Sagoo	NAAL PLAYER/PHOTOGRAPHER/NEW OWNER/RAJ/2ND FAT AUNTIE/HAROLD
Zohra Segal	SPIRIT OF KALI/2ND OFFICIAL/MOTHER IN LAW (DADIMA)/MUSLIM GIRL
Feroza Syal (now Meera Syal)	BIBI/STALLHOLDER/COW IN NATIVITY/ ANITRA/DR MISTRY
Lou Wakefield	PREM/OLD AGE PENSIONER/ROSE/COW IN FIELD/AUCTIONEER

Directed by	Carole Hayman
Designed by	Amanda Fisk
Lighting Designed by	Geoff Mersereau
Choreographed by	Sue Lefton
Costumes by	Pam Tait, Amanda Fisk
Musical Director	Lizzie Kean
Stage Management	Fiona Dyas, Louise Grime, Stephen Rolfe
Publicist	Min Jones
General Manager	Anne Louise Wirgman

First performance: Leicester Haymarket Studio, 15 February 1984
Subsequently: Royal Court Theatre, London, 30 March 1984

Left to right:
Stephanie Fayerman and Peter Sproule.

The Power of the Dog
by Howard Barker

Cast

Sean Baker	POSKREBYSHEV/VICTOR/POLICEMAN
Amelda Brown	RUSSIAN INTERPRETER/MATRIMOVA
Stephanie Fayerman	ILONA
Hugh Fraser	ENGLISH INTERPRETER/SORGE
Tamara Hinchco	WAITER/TREMBLAYEV/GLORIA/DONKIN
Catherine McDonough	WAITER/NEESKIN
Philip McGough	STALIN/GASSOV
Matthew Scurfield	McGROOT/MELANKOV/LASHENKO/TOSHACK
Peter Sproule	CHURCHILL/ARKOV/ZDHANOV/BUBER

Directed by	Kenny Ireland
Designed by	Roger Glossop
Lighting Designed by	Dave Horn
Costumes Designed by	Pam Tait
Costume Assistant	Tina Dalton
Production Manager	Peter Glencross
Production Electrician	Albert J. Tinlin
Stage Manager	Catherine McDonough
Publicist	Nicola Brasher-Jones
General Manager	Anne Louise Wirgman

First performance: Lyceum Studio, Edinburgh, 13 November 1984
Subsequently: Hampstead Theatre Club, London, 22 January 1985

Left to right:
Kathryn Pogson, Tricia Kelly and Paul Jesson. (Photo: Christopher Pearce.)

Deadlines
by Stephen Wakelam
A co-production with the Theatre Upstairs

Workshop group
As production except Paul Mooney replaced Alan David

Cast

Ralph Brown	RAY/MAXWELL/BRAILSFORD/POLICE/JIM
Paul Jesson	TOM/STEVE/HARRY/BARKER/ALEX
Tricia Kelly	HELEN/MAUDIE/GWYN/MEL
Paul Mooney	PATRICK/MAYOR/CHRIS/PETER/SNELLIE
Kathryn Pogson	KATE/LESLEY
Shirin Taylor	LYNN/DI/ANGELA/IRENE/SILK

Directed by	Simon Curtis
Designed by	David Roger
Lighting Designed by	Tom Donnellan
Music by	Andrew Dickson
Sound by	Andy Pink
Production Manager	Simon Byford
Stage Manager (Sheffield/London)	Chris Bagust
Stage Manager (Liverpool/Birmingham)	Peter Glencross
Touring Electrician	Matt Jones
Deputy Stage Manager/ Sound Operator	Fiona Bardsley
Wardrobe Supervisor	Cathie Skilbeck
Publicist	Nicola Brasher-Jones
Voice Coach	Annie Hulley
General Manager	Anne Louise Wirgman

First performance: Crucible Theatre Studio, Sheffield, 21 February 1985
Subsequently: Theatre Upstairs, Royal Court, London, 12 March 1985

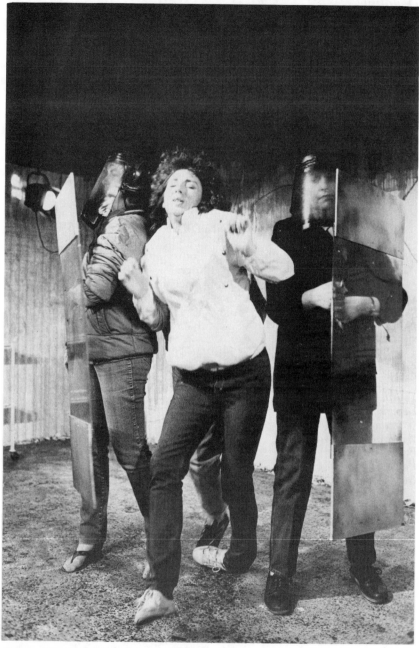

Left to right: Maggie McCarthy, Janette Legge and Rita May.
(Photo: Christopher Pearce.)

Amid the Standing Corn
by Jane Thornton
A co-production with the Soho Poly Theatre

Workshop group
Lindsay Duncan, Deborah Findlay, Carole Hayman, Lesley Manville,
Jane Thornton

Cast

Tracie Bennett	LYNN/BETTY/KEN/BINGO CALLER
Janette Legge	DOT/TERRY/SANDRA/MARIE
Rita May	MAUREEN/ALEC/JERRY/
	POLICEMAN/BINGO CALLER
Maggie McCarthy	MAY/JOAN/GEORGE/HARRY/
	POLICEMAN

Directed by	Carole Hayman
Designed by	Claudia Mayer
Costumes Designed by	Pam Tait
Lighting Designed by	Inigo Espejel
Music by	Helen Ireland
Publicist	Lou Wakefield
Production/Stage Manager	Alan Day
Assistant Stage Manager	Simon Garcha

First performance: Soho Poly Theatre, London, 11 June 1985

Left to right:
Leo Wringer, Vincent Ebrahim and David Howey.
(Photo: Paul Armstrong.)

Fire in the Lake
by Karim Alrawi
Presented in association with Liverpool Playhouse

Workshop group
Karim Alrawi, Amelda Brown, Souad Faress, John Matshikiza, Raad Rawi,
Annie Smart, Jennie Stoller, Andy Treacher, Philip Voss, Jules Wright

Cast

Amelda Brown	RUTH/ZENA
Vincent Ebrahim	DAVID/CHRIS/ALVIN/YAHYA
Souad Faress	HELEN/MAMA SOFIA/JANE ROGERS
David Howey	SAM/KADIR BEY/A MINER
Leo Wringer	FELIX/MAN ON DRIGG DUMP

Directed by	Les Waters
Designed by	Annie Smart
Lighting Designed by	Paul Armstrong
Production Manager	Mark Sainsbury
Stage Managers	Hazel Chrisp, Simon Elson, Simon Richardson, Hazel Ryan
Publicist	Diana Speirs
Administrator	Jennie Matheson

First performance: Theatre Workshop, Edinburgh, 20 August 1985

PART THREE
SELF - REPORT:
NOTES, ESSAYS, ADVENTURES

When and why did the 'underground' happen? What was it? Longer rehearsals, artistic control, long-term formulation of style and policy. Why did it finish? Weariness, small audiences. Was it absorbed into the mainstream? Only sporadically. When we attempted to break through to the middle-ground we couldn't take audiences with us.

The big mistake is that we threw up no real estate. The situation now is that commissions for plays are spread around; new writers are sought after but without much commitment from theatres or the writers themselves: both are just playing the field.

What I miss and lament is: a number of 2/300 seat theatres, a citadel to act as an instigator for new work.

Response: Joint Stock.

Max Stafford-Clark, Notebook, July 1974

If you want to rehearse a play for three or four months you ought to be able to, and not be under pressure to do one every six or seven weeks. But in the big ensembles you are under pressure to turn out seven or eight or more plays a year, and I don't think that kind of repertoire is creating exciting theatre. I think it sometimes produces good theatre, but I don't think anything new ever comes out of that. To create new work you need a different nursery, conditions in which there is total concentration on the play, not on anything else.

Bill Gaskill, Plays and Players, April 1973

David Aukin (producer)

Joint Stock began life in the basement of my then home on St John's Wood Road in London, a house now occupied by Lord Annan, one of the pillars of the intellectual establishment. In retrospect, this now seems splendidly appropriate, for Joint Stock was born with, if not a silver then certainly a brass spoon in its mouth; it was accepted and encouraged almost before it began. Those were the days when the Arts Council had money to dole out to new ventures, and the initial approaches Max Stafford-Clark and I made for funding were met with instant support. Today no one could recognise this as a description of the Arts Council at work, but I am writing of affluent times, although to those of us then on the fringe, they did not seem that affluent.

Our concept of Joint Stock was pure: to provide work on a one-off project basis for those who had been associated with fringe groups. It was to be an umbrella organisation – a phrase that always made Bill Gaskill laugh. There was to be no permanent acting company but merely a modest administrative structure which would enable projects to happen. Initially, this administrative structure was in fact Sonia Hackett who single-handedly tied the company together.

The background to this was that the first tide of the British fringe, inspired by the visits of foreign companies directed by O'Horgan, Beck, Mnouchkine and Chaikin, was ebbing. The energy to run a permanent company without a building base had been exhausted, primarily by touring to arts centres around the country to perform to audiences of twenty or thirty and then arriving in London or at the Edinburgh Festival to be met by the full and concentrated gaze of the critical establishment.

Joint Stock's first show, *The Speakers*, was inspired by a venture in the rooms above the same basement on St John's Wood Road. Max had there seen the Freehold Company under Nancy Meckler's direction perform two acts from *Three Sisters*. The performances happened around our kitchen, sitting-room and study. It's a big house. Entrances were made through the front door, scenes ended and were taken up in another room without any warning to the audience, who wandered around the house picking up the action wherever it had moved. This, confined to one space, became the staging of Heathcote Williams's piece about the Hyde Park Corner speakers.

The shift in the company's policy that occurred when Max, Bill and David Hare were working on *Fanshen* was obviously a turning point. Sitting around in a circle in the rehearsal room, the company examined its own structure and organisation, and concluded that the company belonged to the co-operative of actors, directors, designers and administrators; no longer would Max or Bill or David or I be responsible as 'management' for running the company and deciding the projects. This would be done by the collective, and, quite uniquely possibly, for this country at least, a formula was developed whereby the company would function as a shifting collective; the current company would be responsible for setting up the next project and, like a chain letter, the next company would do likewise.

More extraordinarily, the company that had been set up to have no defined style, indeed to embrace a diversity of styles and talents, rapidly developed its own distinctive house-style, a style that came through, whatever the composition of the group. Clearly there was an element of it being a self-perpetuating house-style, with the incumbents instinctively handing on to those who shared a similar approach and taste, and importantly, could be relied on to hand it back. Nothing wrong with that.

On the contrary, the strength of Joint Stock was that it abandoned its original objectives as it developed an approach to theatre, to its material, to the work process, which provided its artistic unity. The question the company must now investigate, and answer, is whether that same drive still exists. Has it become institutionalised and continues merely because it is there? Has the company today the same flexibility to respond to new ideas or will it go on producing merely because the subsidy and structure exist? The next productions will be time enough to test these questions, and when the moment comes to wind it up, as it surely one day will, this decision will be examined with the clarity and lack of sentimentality that Joint Stock applies to all its work.

Tony Bicât (writer)

My first contact with Joint Stock was a meeting at David Aukin's house in 1973. This was shortly after the end of Portable Theatre. It was thought that there might be some virtue in the new Company, then without a name, taking over the shard of the Limited Company David Hare and myself had set up in 1968 for Portable. I pointed out that both the name and the debts of Portable would be a millstone round the new Company's neck and that since we now only spoke to the Arts Council through our solicitor, any goodwill we may have had there had evaporated. I was asked if I wanted to have anything to do with the new Company. I replied that I never wanted to have anything to do with the theatre again as long as I lived.

Bill Gaskill (director)

I don't know why Max Stafford-Clark, David Aukin and David Hare founded Joint Stock. I was not involved in it. I admired Max's work at the Traverse and I had brought his workshop company to the Royal Court (which I ran from 1965 to 1972) for several visits. David Hare had been my literary manager ('exploited', as he said during the *Fanshen* workshop, on £7 10s. a week, though by that time he was the richest 'peasant' in the group.) David Aukin I didn't know.

Max and I were sitting on the steps of the Royal Court one day in 1973 talking about the future – or so my memory of it is. Max had given up his Traverse company and I had left the Court; we both knew – and liked – each other's work but not our working methods. We decided we would have a workshop in which we demonstrated our exercises, improvisations and rehearsal methods with a group of actors invited by us. Nobody was to be paid and we were not necessarily planning a production after the workshop. We agreed that we should take a text to focus the work and I suggested Heathcote Williams *The Speakers*, which was first given to me by Harold Pinter. Heathcote had written *A/C, D/C* for the Court where it had a trendy success in 1971.

We started work in the Abbey Community Centre in Marsham Street in the autumn of 1973, with a large-ish group of actors some of whom soon left, some of whom, like Tony Rohr and Paul Freeman, became the backbone of Joint Stock in the years ahead. I don't remember many of the exercises I used. Max showed me a lot of 'trust' exercises – walking blindfold through a room full of tintacks guided only by the whispers of a colleague; jumping off a rostrum into the waiting arms of the group – most of these picked up, I guess, from Max's time with La Mama in New York. There were many exercises on speaking on any subject for specified lengths of time, subjects not known to the speaker, like Staffordshire Pottery or the Albigensian Heresy. We did this every day as a verbal gymnastic preparation for playing the speakers in Heathcote's book – a documentary recording of four actual speakers in Hyde Park in about 1963. Different actors chose speakers from the book to work on, both in their public speeches and in the scenes from their private lives which Heathcote had invaded. Interestingly, the writer was not at the workshop or significantly in the rehearsal period, as was later to be standard Joint Stock practice.

At the end of the workshop Max and I decided to go ahead with a dramatisation of the book and we applied for a project grant from the Arts Council. We divided the book into units, to each of which we gave a title, occasionally flippant – 'Van Dyn's Boring Stories' – occasionally poetic – 'The Silent Man Speaks' – and wrote them down on slips of paper which we juggled to make a structure. The book is made up of an opening and closing section in the park and an individual chapter on each of the four speakers. We decided to eliminate one of the speakers and to intercut the other three in a mosaic. The first text was literally the book cut into pieces and pasted together, more like a film script than a play.

We started work straight after Christmas 1973.

The first rehearsal was in the Mother Redcap in Camden Town. Max and I had decided to co-direct the show which could have made for difficulties. In fact it worked like a dream and was the basis of the next two productions – *Fanshen* and *Yesterday's News*, and had a significant influence on the development of Joint Stock. It could never have the personal stamp of one director like Pip Simmons or most of the fringe groups. Sometimes there were problems. We used to divide up the scenes involving different actors and rehearse them in different corners of the room. At the end of the day we would show each other the work we had done, discuss it and change over the following day. (The segmented structure of the play lent itself to this.) At the end of one day Oliver Cotton was going through one of his speeches standing on a chair; at the end of his peroration he fell in what should have been a spectacular way but in fact was rather a naff way. In the notes session, thinking this to be an invention of Max's, I started rather tentatively, 'about the fall . . .'; 'Yes', said Max, eqaully cautiously, 'I don't care for it . . . .' It turned out to have been an addition of Oliver's. But the process worked well.

This simultaneous rehearsal in the same space mirrored the physical shape the production was to take. Very early on we had decided that at least part of the show would be a recreation of Speakers' Corner with the audience moving around in what is now known as a promenade manner and the actors vieing for the attention of the audience just as the real-life speakers did. We were by this time back in the Abbey Community Centre, where we did the first preview of the show. The speakers spoke from the centres of the four sides of the room, the scenes outside Hyde Park were played in the four corners. Max had the idea that there should be a permanent tea-stall, manned by Freddie Kilennen, actually serving tea, and I said it should be in the centre of the space. Andy Phillips, the lighting designer, had a brilliant idea for the lighting; the board operator would be based on a platform built on a scaffolding tower above the tea stall; he would operate a follow-spot on which a miniature lighting board was mounted so that he could operate both at once; there were four tungsten halogen lamps (an idea pinched from Peter Brook) which illuminated the whole area with a flat light for all the scenes in the park; the corners were lit by specials and the follow-spot could contract right down for private moments like Tony Rohr's white face speaking McGuinness's thoughts surrounded by darkness. The movement of the audience was controlled by the lighting – sometimes they could wander freely, sometimes they had to listen to one person. Eventually we also overlapped some of the interior scenes by bringing light up on one scene before another had finished. This caught the dream-like nature of Heathcote's documentary recording and made what might have been a slice-of-life into something poetic.

Roger Lloyd Pack (actor)

I remember visiting Max Stafford-Clark's flat in the summer of 1973. Max asked me what I thought was the best name for a theatre company – Joint Stock or Rolling Stock. In front of him were several pictures of locomotives and old steam engines. Joint Stock, he told me, had to do with the amalgamation of carriages on the old North British line. I smiled. I preferred Rolling Stock myself. If Max hadn't been a director he would have been good casting for an engine driver. As it turned out, he made a very passable roadie. On *The Speakers* tour we did varying night stands in Brighton, Birmingham, Lancaster and Nottingham, playing in rudimentary spaces which we converted to our own ends, staying in less than luxurious lodging houses (a vicious alsation greeted us one night after the show), travelling in a 15cwt blue Ford van.

I had actually turned down the offer to take part in the original workshops. They were unpaid. I desperately needed money and had been offered £150 to paint somebody's flat. However, after a rough script had been assembled, I managed to infiltrate myself into the company to play Harry. There was a strong cast. It was a tremendously exciting and daunting prospect. What? Speak directly to the audience and have them walk around us, wherever they wanted? Who had heard of such a thing? I was used to the audience sitting still, in one place.

Rehearsals were at once exhilarating and intimidating. We did a lot of exercises in public speaking, speaking persistently on different subjects for set lengths of time, being heckled by other members of the company. The crazy and eccentric life of these obsessional heroes dominated our days and invaded our being. We roamed around the rehearsal room above a pub in Camden Town, watched, hawk-eyed, by Bill, magisterial and austere, and Max, coaxing and encouraging. Heathcote flitted about, rarely still, dispensing wisdom. 'You have to have a home. You go mad without a home.' Few of these people we were playing had homes. Not that they could call their own. A new approach to acting was needed to suit the context, a certain kind of reality is demanded when you are talking to your audience only a few feet away, a certain kind of truth. Actually it's the same truth you seek in all acting, but here it was distilled, in close up. 'It's not a question of good or bad. Is it an experience?' You don't get away with very much with Bill.

The first performance we gave to an invited group of theatrical friends and luminaries was the most unnerving experience I have ever had in the theatre. We were engaged in this new way of working which made us feel particularly vulnerable, uncertain how it would work, and everywhere I looked there were people I knew and was in awe of. Whenever I am frightened now, before a first night, I think back to that evening and am reassured that nothing, nothing, can ever be as bad as that. But, after a bit of fiddling about, it worked. It was triumphant and, sometimes, electric. It broke new ground and old barriers. The audience became part of the show. In Birmingham I had a cup of tea thrown in my face. There was a stall in the middle of the acting area where people could buy tea and biscuits. I had a line, 'Nothing you can do or say can startle me in any shape or form.' Whoosh! An elderly lady discharges the remains of her tea in my face. I carry on, trying hard not to look surprised. Later, in a quiet moment, I seek this woman out and ask her why she did it. 'I've always wanted to do it, that's why. And I've never done it.' In Nottingham when, as a policeman, I had to clear the park (audience) at the end, two men challenged my right to do this and started to argue with me, got on our soap boxes and started to harangue the departing crowd. 'Who does this policeman think he is? He can't get rid of us. We can stay if we want to.' 'Look,' I said finally, 'I'm only an actor. It's only a show.' At the ICA in London I exchanged phone numbers with a woman who wanted to paint my portrait. I sustained a conversation with her in character. Things like this happened a lot of the time. We were also heckled. People would get drunk and join in the show, shouting back at the speakers and challenging us. The actors were always on the line. In Amsterdam the audiences went wild. The company went a little off the rails as well. It was 1974. Amsterdam. What could you expect? Back in England, regular meetings began to establish a working method and a way of monitoring the progress of the company. And more meetings. Joint Stock is now famous for its work and famous for its meetings. But there seems to be an organic cell within the company that ensures that it is changing all the time, adapting itself to itself, constantly re-examining and questioning the work.

A critic at *The Speakers*

PRESENTER: Did you feel tempted to take part in the proceedings, Margaret Drabble?

MARGARET DRABBLE: No, I didn't feel at all tempted. I wouldn't have been tempted at Hyde Park either though. I found this an interesting evening, but not at all an enjoyable one. In fact, I found it rather exhausting and I'd advise people to take

strong shoes. One walks around rather a lot during the
course of the evening.

PRESENTER: Or a shooting stick.

MARGARET DRABBLE: Or a shooting stick. A shooting stick would be
the best thing one could possibly take. I found it turning into
rather a competition to find somewhere to sit down to watch
the next bit of the action.

(Radio Three, *Critics' Forum*)

Bill Gaskill (director)

The success of *The Speakers* and the pleasure we all had in working together
made another show inevitable. We would apply for a revenue grant from the
Arts Council. Already the idea of workshop-gap-rehearsal, which with a few
exceptions was to become standard, was planned. We had also made it
an article of faith to have a long rehearsal period, not less than six weeks,
and that we would say to the Arts Council that this was essential to maintain
the quality of the work. Fortunately, we were so successful that they
accepted this.

What was the new show to be? We had a meeting of the group in my flat –
the first of many in which the actors were involved in decision-making. The
suggestions included: something about Nijinsky (Toby Salaman), the
Bloomsbury group (Paul Freeman); an adaptation of John Cowper Powys' *A
Glastonbury Romance* (Roderic Leigh); *Play* by Jeff Nuttall (Cecily Hobbs,
who had replaced Jennie Stoller); Flann O'Brien's *At Swim Two Birds* (the
inevitable Rohr). I can't remember what Max suggested but the choices give
some idea of the relics of late sixties taste prevalent in the group. In spite of
popular belief we were not a politically committed ensemble.

My suggestion was William Hinton's epic book about revolution in a
Chinese village, *Fanshen*, which had been recommended to me by Pauline
Melville – not at that time a member of the group – and it was this that was
eventually decided on. I approached David Hare about adapting it and, rather
to my surprise, he agreed. The night before we were due to start the workshop
I rang up Max and proposed that all decisions made about the work should be
made communally to reflect the character of the book. Rather grudgingly he
agreed. Joint Stock was about to become politicised.

David Hare (writer)

I've been involved in founding two theatre companies in my life. The first,
Portable Theatre, ended for me in the Marylebone Magistrates Court some
time, I believe, in 1973. I kept no diary in those days – I was young, and
events moved so slowly – so I have no way of remembering. I do know I
shook and sweated a great deal, since I'd only learned on the morning of my
appearance that Tony Bicât and I would have to appear in court. The charge
was non-payment of actors' National Insurance Stamps. Since we had
relinquished the running of the company some time previously, we were both
surprised to find ourselves still legally responsible for its present state –
although, to be fair, I had recently seen its administrator at Schiphol Airport

in Amsterdam drinking gin at seven-thirty in the morning, and might have
guessed that the books were not in too solid a shape. The magistrate fined us
– was it £35? I misremember – and ordered us to pay all our debts. When the
company later went bankrupt, we learned that your debt to the state is the one
debt that can never be absolved.

Things have changed a great deal in theatre in the last fifteen years. In those
easier days you needed less money to start a new company, and everyone
accepted that theatres might naturally flower and die. The fringe had not been
institutionalized to the point where companies fear to relinquish grants from
the Arts Council long after their artistic life has been exhausted.

Max Stafford-Clark, David Aukin and I met among the ruins of Portable
Theatre and decided that since we were all freelance members of the awkward
squad, we were likely to need our own facility for putting on plays. All our
experience had been with the presentation of new work, usually of a modestly
controversial kind, and we were all well aware of how producers' expectations
then rarely fitted either with our personalities or our tastes. I went away, to be
honest, with little intention of using that facility – struck much more by the
way Max, unknowable then as now, was going through a phase of insisting
that there was too much snobbery in the world about what people ate and
drank. To prove his point, he created Joint Stock in conversation while
drinking large schooners of viscous sweet sherry.

For a while we seemed to choose plays which we rehearsed and presented
in the regular way, although our bent was for the pornographic. (One of our
shows was later to be debated in the House of Lords, where its artistic merit
was vigorously contested.) But unknown to me, Max had begun talking to Bill
Gaskill about doing a period of work on Heathcote Williams's book *The
Speakers*, with no specific intention of showing the result to the public. I was
therefore surprised when I met Bill in the street one day and he remarked
ironically on the fact that, as a member of the three-man Joint Stock board, I
was now his employer. Only five years previously I had been the greenest
recruit to his celebrated regime at the Royal Court.

When in 1974 Max and Bill finally decided to show their work to friends in
a rehearsal-room in Westminster, I was taken aback. The directors had
re-created Hyde Park Corner by simply upturning a few boxes and asking the
audience to wander freely from speaker to speaker. The evening appeared to
be casual, and yet turned out to be highly structured. There was a great
density of characterisation. (In fact, I believe when the 'real' speakers came to
see themselves impersonated, they were perfectly satisfied.) Since the play
appeared on the surface to be plotless, there was none of the usual wrenching
and shifting of gears to which a playwright's ears are especially attuned. There
was nothing flashy or insincere. The evening was dry, in the best sense, like
good wine. I had long known it to be Bill's aim as a director to achieve work
in which the content of the play was in perfect relief – there was to be no
impression of artifice – and yet often in the past I had felt the very austerity
of his approach to be mannered. Now, perhaps because his talents allied
exquisitely with Max's gift for detail, the audience was actually presented with
the illusion of meeting and getting to know the speakers at Hyde Park Corner.
No more, no less. The speakers were in the round, unforced, *themselves*.

All three of us suspected that the main reason for the evening's success had been the absence of a writer. The directors had cut the pages from Heathcote Williams's book, which had provided the dialogue for the play, into slivers on the floor with a big pair of scissors. There was a general feeling, perhaps brought on by Max and Bill's recent directorships of writers' theatres, that writers always spoil things. Both the greatest English directors of the post-war theatre, Peter Brook and Joan Littlewood, had ended up without writers in their rehearsal rooms. Pauline Melville had lent Bill a copy of William Hinton's massive book *Fanshen* and the very impossibility of adapting it appealed to him. Yet he passed it on to me with a poorly disguised heavy heart.

A particular tension in Joint Stock has never been very satisfactorily resolved. Writers have a reputation for being tied to one view of the world – their own – but in experimental work actors and directors must feel free. The actor wants to own his character. The director wants to control the evening. The company has been at its most successful either when using writers with very strong personalities – Caryl Churchill, say, or Barrie Keeffe – or when working on shows in which the writer appears to stand out of the way of the raw material altogether. In *Yesterday's News* a group of actors sat facing the audience, using transcripts of interviews which they had secured themselves with British mercenaries who had been in Angola. The same technique served in *Falkland Sound*, a Joint Stock show in all but name, half of which is made up from letters sent by David Tinker to his father from a ship in the expeditionary force, and half of which dramatizes, in their own words, the lives of people caught up in the Falklands War. Both plays, although apparently documentary, were more artful than they at first appeared. The company's touch was less sure when playwrights were compromised somewhere in the middle, not quite knowing whether to set down the actors' research, or to try and create a play of their own. With *Fanshen* Bill had little choice, for the book is nearly 700 pages long and playwrights, for all their faults, are good men with pickaxes.

Hinton is a Pennsylvania farmer who was in China for six years as a tractor technician. *Fanshen* records the life and struggles of the people in the village of Long Bow during the great land reform programmes which Mao's revolution instituted in the late 1940s. I worked on trying to digest and master the extraordinary complexity of the book, while, in workshop, the actors flung themselves at whatever bit they fancied, more or less in whatever style they fancied. The writer represented reason, the actors imagination. There were certainly masks in the rehearsal room, and there was talk of puppet shows. Stylization was much discussed. At one point, I was asked to play a bird. It was important to the directors that the method of workshop reflect the subject and that it therefore be genuinely democratic. For that reason Bill once insisted as we returned from lunch to our basement rehearsal room in Pimlico that neither he, Max nor I should be the ones to suggest resuming work that afternoon. We would simply wait until an actor suggested it. I think we waited about an hour and a half.

After the workshop I went off by myself and spent four months mining a text out of the book. I threw away a great deal of the more obviously dramatic material, because I was not interested in portraying the scenes of violence and brutality which marked the landlords' regime and its overthrow. In shaping the play, I was very little influenced by any particular discovery in the workshop, but I was crucially affected by its spirit. Although Bill had thrashed about seeking to find a suitable style for the work, often lapsing into long and sullen silences, he never relaxed his basic intention: that we should do justice to the sufferings of the Chinese peasants. This was a matter of the utmost gravity to him. His criterion for examining any scene was to ask whether it was adequate to the experience the peasant had originally undergone. Although the subject-matter of the play was political, the instincts of the company were in essence moral. We were not revolutionaries. I think that is why, especially in later seasons when it sought to apply the lessons of *Fanshen* to English material, Joint Stock became confused about whether it was a political group or not. In making *Fanshen*, none of us believed we could duplicate the over-turning we described. We knew any form of change here was bound to be different. But we all admired the revolution, and shared an obligation to describe it in a way of which its people would approve. The adoption of a rehearsal process based on the Chinese political method of 'Self-Report, Public Appraisal' might, in other hands and with other material, have degenerated into a gimmick. But here it had weight and was surprisingly quick and effective. The self-criticism was real.

At Christmas I finished, and a few days later was sitting beside my wife's hospital bed when Bill breezed in from two weeks with the aborigines in Australia. He took one uninterested look at our two-day-old son and said, 'Yes. Very nice. Where's the play?' Soon after he arranged a reading with the whole company. It was very long and lugubrious, and at the end people said almost nothing, though one actor shook his head at me and said 'Sorry'. Given the general gloom, I had no idea why I was not asked to rewrite much more. Only the beginning was rearranged and somewhat peremptorily. If I had been more experienced, of course, I would have recognised that moment at which a group of people, expecting everything, are delivered something.

The play opened in Sheffield in April 1975 to a refreshingly intelligent and multi-racial audience, then came to London. I was on a beach in Greece when word came that I was needed at once to work on a television version. Hinton had hitherto ignored the whole production assuming that, like the two previous dramatic versions, ours would disappear without trace. But when he read the reviews, he appeared in England almost at once. He consulted with his daughter, who had been a Red Guard, and then with officials from the Chinese Embassy, before insisting that the play must be altered if its life was to be prolonged. The BBC flew me back to his farm to argue with him, and I found him waiting with a list of 110 changes, most of which sought to i. . the play of what he called – I am using shorthand here – my 'liberal' slant and to give it more of what I would call his 'Marxist' emphasis. An exceptionally generous and decent man, he proved a wonderful host, even as we set out on two days of attritional argument, which resulted in my once or twice giving the play a slightly more optimistic tilt. A line about justice which I had hitherto believed to be the fulcrum was removed. The play still stood. If I ever felt resentful about this, I only had to remind myself that his notes had twice been seized, once by the US Customs and then again by the Senate. The writing of the book had taken him fifteen years. I had given barely six months.

The television version was, in my view at least, something of a fiasco. I had an early bet with Bill that I would give him a shilling for every time the BBC director said 'no' to anything which was suggested to him. After all the pain and profound argument we had had about how best to represent a revolution on stage, we were now in the hands of a man who believed that all you had to do to televise a play was to point a camera at it. Bill told me not to be ridiculous, but at the end I didn't have to pay him a penny.

Subsequently *Fanshen* was revived whenever Joint Stock was in trouble. It became our *Mousetrap*. Once, humiliatingly, I attempted to do a couple of days' directing one of its many revivals and found it to be a lot less easy than it seemed. Although I thought I understood the process whereby Max and Bill had done their work, in practice I was hopeless at imitating even their most casual effects. The spirit of the show was best guarded by actors like Paul Freeman and David Rintoul.

The two directors and I sought many times to work together again as a team. I asked Bill to direct a couple of my plays, but he always turned me down. We all found it hard to imagine material which would suit us as well. In part this was because *Fanshen* describes a period of history in which people's lives were unarguably improved: when someone suggested we do a similar show about the Russian revolution I pointed out that it was quite hard, in view of what we all knew happened later, to bring the same relish to describing the heady days of 1918. It would have been dishonest. We tried to acquire the rights to Studs Terkel's *Working*. When it subsequently flopped as a musical on Broadway, Studs asked us to reconsider, but the moment had gone. I worked listlessly on Tolstoy's *Resurrection*, only to be told by Bill that I was getting nowhere. I headed instead to run my own workshop with Tony Bicât as my writer. I tried, for once, to work on less political material. But I lacked Bill and Max's flair for letting things run away of their own accord. Later, however, a friend was driving from Stratford to London with Trevor Nunn, who was about to do a workshop of *Nicholas Nickleby*. 'I have no idea what a workshop is,' Nunn was saying, 'I've never done one. Can you give me any idea what David does?'

Joint Stock, inspired by *Fanshen*, then chose to go co-operative, and all decisions were taken by group discussion. The actors were brought in to help run the company. Some fine work followed, and for two years they managed both to maintain a high standard of performance and to attract a large and dedicated audience. Usually the characterisation had much more quirkiness and vitality than we had managed in *Fanshen*. Both Howard Brenton's *Epsom Downs* and Barrie Keeffe's *A Mad World, My Masters* had much more gaiety. And yet you sensed that the principles of the work were the same as those we had forged when trying to do a play about China. Although the subject-matter changed, the ideology became a little stuck. I suppose I reluctantly concluded that an openly political way of working only pays off with dialectical material.

I stopped going to company meetings after a group discussion in which I called someone a cunt. Although I was referring to somebody who wasn't present, I was told by one of the group that she objected to my using a piece of her anatomy as a term of abuse. I replied fatuously that it had hardly been *her* anatomy in particular which I had had in mind. Of course she was right, and I have never again used the word as an insult, although it remains the one English swear-word with a genuine power to shock. Yet somehow the incident oppressed me disproportionately. An actor made a long speech about how the only purpose of theatre now must be to work for the overthrow of the

Thatcher government, then left as soon as his best friend arrived to have a separate conversation in the garden. He had actually cried during the speech. The politics of gesture seemed to have replaced the politics of need. Now we were all to have silly arguments about words.

Of all art forms the theatre is most susceptible to fashion. There is good and bad in this. There are times at which audiences seem to respond to an idea, almost irrespective of how well or badly it is expressed, as if it is already in the air, and nothing will now stop them getting to it. All of us sensed that happening with *Fanshen*, and the actors and directors worked to some common imperative. Nobody was frightened. This is not the only kind of theatre I wish to work in, but the feeling has come upon me only twice, and the first time was with Joint Stock.

(This article appeared in *Granta*, May 1986)

Carole Hayman (actress)

I remember . . .

Suggesting the Board consider more projects by women and being told there were no plays by women because women had nothing to write about – they hadn't *done* anything in the world.

Learning T'ai Chi.

Meetings that seemed to last four days.

Complaining about the size of the women's parts in *Fanshen* and the distribution of them and being told men ran the revolution not women; and anyway it would tax our imagination enough learning how to play a Chinese peasant.

Self-criticism. Always ended in a slanging match.

Fleas in the rehearsal room carpet.

Max Stafford-Clark (director)

The following edited extracts are from notebooks I kept between August 1974 and May 1975 and cover the workshop of *Fanshen* and the rehearsals leading up to the first performance. They're certainly not comprehensive nor do they reflect any individual's real contribution. I tended to write most often at moments of frustration or boredom and times of excitement often went unrecorded. My recollection of the workshop period is of the earnest attempts we made to grapple with a culture that was so far removed from our own, not just politically but in every nuance of behaviour. I remember Ken Cranham giggling and saying, 'We're not going to start with peasants hoeing, are we, just to show how poor we are?' 'Oh no,' we reassured him, but that's of course exactly what we did do. Not the least of David Hare's achievements was to mirror our struggles with the material to the cadres' struggles in bringing Communism to Long Bow.

We started rehearsal of David Hare's text in January 1975. The work was split between the two directors: to begin with we rehearsed different scenes simultaneously in different parts of the hall but as rehearsal progressed this became less possible and we would split the day between us, one director taking the morning session and the other taking over in the afternoon. I recall only one sharp disagreement between Bill and I which was over some detail of the 'Division of Spoils' scene. My main recollection is of the excitement of seeing work I had done carried further and fresh possibilities opening up. Bill made the early running and I recall the sculptural detail with which scenes were shaped. Surprisingly late in rehearsal (the fifth week?) I caught on to the dialectical method and was able to refocus whole scenes and characters by taking decisions based on the political line of the play – and not on how each actor thought his character would behave in a particular situation. Bill came in late one morning and sat watching. At lunchtime he took me aside and said how good it was and urged me to keep working through his afternoon session. It was a day of heady elation that went totally unremarked in these notebooks.

20 August	**First day of workshop.** Spent the whole day discussing whether we were to be a democratic body. In the end we decided we were. Big deal. Talk, talk, talk. Submit to process but no great faith in it as a working-method.
21 August	When will we stop talking and do something? Trouble is nobody quite knows where to begin. Go over details of story in book. Extremely tedious. Rather like an awful school exam.
22 August	Story-telling of life in China before the war – very remote and did not sound very personal, so then tried telling stories which were much closer to our own cultural experience. Degenerated into talk again. Another frustrating day.
23-26 August	Classification of company (based on classification of the peasants by the peasants themselves to determine who should receive what in the New Society). How much did Pauline's husband earn last year? What percentage did Bill receive from his West End transfer? Did he 'grind the faces of the poor' – his employees – when director of the Royal Court? Does Ken lead a dissipated existence? Was he irresponsible to turn down *Henry IV* at Nottingham because he didn't like the tavern scenes? Did Cecily need material help? How much longer could Roger expect to live rent-free? What was Oliver's mortgage? What about Toby's family background etc? It's all a process of finding out.
27 August	Begin with T'ai Chi/ Very nice. Spend the day acting out a meeting, a share-out meeting for those poor peasants who had not 'fanshened'. Still the same basic problems; (a) lack of familiarity with text and material; (b) totally alien nature of Chinese. Trying to be them when you can bring nothing of your own cultural associations to the exercise. English acting depends a great deal on the nuances of class difference and suddenly none of that is relevant.

28 August   Mask work with Roderic. Parable about enlarging the
Communist Party. Roderic trying to isolate the actions – Bill
explains that actions alone can advance the story. Obviously
there is a scene here. A play within a play seems a better idea
than ever. A bit of directorial conflict. 'It's not finished,'
says Roderic. 'It is,' says Bill. Very hard. We can't all
direct at once.

29 August   Transformation exercise. Two people discover for themselves
what status is, changing from high to low status – i.e. boss
to secretary (GB), husband to wife (China). With masks
and without.

30 August   Self-criticism. Paul criticised me for being too bossy and
wanting to take over Carole's exercise.
    Bill's exercise on actions. 'I am a ticket collector, I collect
tickets' etc.' Describe the actions and then do them. 'You
should not avoid the obvious,' said Bill.

1 September   Main difficulty is still relating to the material and finding
some way of getting into a subject that we don't have
much instinctive sympathy and understanding for, or much
knowledge of.
    Part of the problem is that we have no collective purpose in
undertaking the show and not even a cohesive and united idea
about what theatre should be like.

2 September   Bill directing a scene David has written.
    'Is it naturalistic?' asks Carole.
    'We'll find out as we go along,' says Bill.
    David made the point he would like to go on writing scenes
and facing the actors with them. The problems of presentation
technique could equally well be solved by rehearsing a scene as
by rehearsing techniques. People felt the workshop should stay
alive and not go into a rehearsal situation.
    Must find a way of depicting violence.

4 September   A very good day. The discussion revealed a common area of
concern and interest in the attitudes to the book.

5 September   Slogans. Exercise to illustrate a slogan.
    'Unite real friends, attack real enemies.'
    'Can the sun rise in the west?' etc.
    Archetypes do work, but it must be more subtle than that.

9 September   Men playing women, and women men.

10 September Women before and after *Fanshen*, and our own situation.
    Discussion about Chineseness and how we could get those
qualities. Max: want to work from ourselves in, i.e. anything
must be approached from the standpoint of ourselves. Whereas
Bill thinks authenticity or as near as possible is desirable.

12 September Simultaneous improvisations of family life in separate parts of
the room. Well in centre where girls meet and talk.

17 September Life in Long Bow improvisations. Beginning the day, chores, jobs etc. Begins to look good for opening section. Marty working in the fields very good because its usualness was established.

20 September Ideas for structure of eventual piece.

Toby: Starting from ourselves and being Chinese, but being first seen as 'Actors'.

David: Purity of ideas contrasted with the particularity of people's lives.

Bill: Problems can be solved by thought, application and practice.

Pauline: Difference between presenting the story and endeavouring to transform the audience so they accept it.

Oliver: Nobody knows nothing about China. We would be educating them.

Is there a show here at all?

Have we worked in the most efficient way?

Has it been much help to David?

28 January **First day of rehearsal.** Questions about theatre as if the rest of us were Chinese.

'In your country is an actor not considered essential and therefore paid less?'

'Is the audience allowed to criticise the actors after the show?'

Developed mimes first in an English context, then Chinese. All were downward-looking, depressed. Bill: 'We've got to feel that as a basis for the work. I don't mind if it's boring.'

Beware we don't comment too much on how miserable and empty their lives are by dull and slow acting rhythms.

29 January Bill: 'The facts are important, but the imagination is even more important.' I talk about danger of making it too glum, too dull. Argument about forms of staging. Me trying it in a kind of Grotowski walkway – public stage arrangement which Bill objected to and thought too complex.

30 January Argument about form of staging continued. Rather sharp disagreement between me and Bill about need for discussion at all. Part of the problem is some people would like to do the show at Wembley and some in the Old Traverse. Some didn't want to do the show on the 'smelly fringe'. Would a production suitable for touring to small theatres also be good for the Young Vic? Are we doing an epic about a national movement or an intimate play about life in a particular village? Akenfield Chinoise or sweet and sour Akenfield? David H. feels the former. I suppose he's right.

3 February Bill asking further questions about background and daily life of individual peasants.

Do we need props? 'If you had only one prop what would it be?'

Roderic: 'Oh, my hoe'; David R: 'My rifle'; Toby: 'A pipe'.

4 February   A good morning. Best thing were interior monologues about what they wanted out of the spoils.

Bill: 'Don't drop your ceiling of ignorance too low on emotional temperature – unless there was a boiling point, how could there have been a revolution at all?

Point Bill is working and driving towards is a greater feeling and experience of just how bad conditions were.

Bill: 'You all feel you have to explain things. Just be there and feel it.'

6 February   'Division of Spoils' scene which was particularly vivid.

Toby was upset yesterday because Bill kept stopping the rehearsal before they could get into it. Watching it again now one can see that it's quite true. Again!

'Too quick, Toby.'

'What's too quick?'

'The walk . . .'

In fact I had liked it enormously.

9 February   Lost Toby.

11 February   Opening should be simpler. Whether or not they're actors, they're not writers. One juicy fact each.

Don't like props at all. Would be better miming it.

12 February   I'm finding things pretty difficult too. How can you rehearse when Bill changes everything one found yesterday. I think I'm going to leave too. Absolute misunderstanding about what rehearsal is for. I was using it for finding impulse of scene. Bill was using it, he said, for props.

Got over it a bit. A few basic questions have got to be sorted out though.

14 February   Role of women not clear. Role of crowds not clear either. Big problem: how you do the speeches. Too emotional.

22 February   Hardship of people must be set up clearer at the very start. Why it is important is because that is what made the revolution possible.

5 March   Run through.

Bill: 'Work and work and work until you're absolutely certain of what you are saying.'

'I have cast doubts on Comrade Hou's dots, but not on his full stops.'

'Be more wooden.'

10 March   Sheffield. Dress rehearsal.
Jane in tears. Starting late. Will we finish by 5.15?
Obviously not.
First performance.
Scene 5: 'All-out war'. Audience beginning to fidget for first
time. This is a key scene . . .

31 April   **Meeting with actors (about next project)**
Bill: 'There is one area we cannot get into and that is rough
theatre. I feel temperamentally unsuited to rough theatre.'
Pip: 'I would like to be a star.'
Everybody: 'Then go anywhere else.'
Pauline: 'I think Joint Stock should do things relevant to
people's lives.'
Tony M.: 'Has anybody read *The Sheep Are Still Grazing*.'
Pip: 'I would like to do a show with music and dancing and
having a good time.'
Max: 'Well, it's called pantomime and it happens every year.'
Tony R.: 'My agent said *Fanshen* was too political.'

9 May   **Session with William Hinton (author of *Fanshen*)**
'Cut out the word "absolute" throughout the script.'
'You don't "summon" people. Too commandist.'
'A peasant would never say "I hate China."' Well that's
true. But as a dramatic point it's good for the play.
'Collaborators should be "executed" not "murdered".'
'"I love the Communist Party as I love my wife" is strong
for an English audience, but no Chinese would say in public
that he loved his wife. They would express love for children or
the community but not their wives.'
'The violence of the Old Society is only talked about but the
violence of the New Society is shown.' Clearly Hinton feels the
necessity to tread the official line that there was little violence
or that violence was eliminated.
Hinton found the atmosphere of bourgeois competitiveness in
the self-criticism scene unacceptable. Very un-Chinese.
Criticism must be more positive and advance the play more.
'Socialist realism is to me the consciousness that life might
change, a consciousness of a new world being born where
bourgeois competitiveness is eliminated.'

10 May   **Actors' reactions**
Pauline: 'I came to *Fanshen* back to front not because I
wanted a job but because I want to do things I see around me.
In a factory or theatre I always want to change things. And I
do not know where best to place myself to carry that out.'
Bill: 'Pauline's contribution to the play was very important
but I would not like to do the play with people entirely
like her.'

Tony R.: 'I've become much more critical about other work I do. I feel a certain loss when I go outside this company.'

Paul: 'That's dangerous too. Have we the courage to commit ourselves? Joint Stock annoys me a lot. Why was there two weeks off in the middle? – Another cock-up.'

Roderic: 'I have a certain amount of energy and a great deal of idealism but I do not find Joint Stock absorbs all my energy.'

Philip: '*Fanshen* was very satisfying emotionally and intellectually and it forced me to be more disciplined as an actor. But I do not mind if the next show is not political.'

Tony M.: 'Are we really playing to a coterie audience in London? I think not.'

Roderic: 'Success has turned it into a cultural event.'

Bill: 'Your attitude is what has turned it into a success together with the way Max and I have staged it.'

Pip: 'Half a co-operative is worse than a whole co-operative.'

Bill: 'I feel the attempt towards democracy has been worthwhile.'

Roderic: 'Could we push it further?'

Max: 'Only if we were going to form a unified group.'

Bill: 'Can I make a confession? At the moment I feel very close and warm towards you all. When I am away from you I do not feel that.'

Pauline Melville (actress)

St Gabriel's Church Hall in Pimlico contains a set of dingy, draughty, large, under-lit and badly heated rehearsal rooms. Each time I've worked with Joint Stock, part or all of the workshop and rehearsal periods have taken place there. Those gloomy rooms contain the ghosts of many Joint Stock productions, actors, writers and directors combining to create often the most extraordinary improvisations, transformations and imaginative work. For the actors, the workshop period is an unusual opportunity to explore styles and approaches to the subject matter; to expand, experiment and discuss, before focusing in on a text during the rehearsal period. Unlike most ordinary rehearsals where actors slope off to have a cigarette and a coffee while the scenes they aren't in are being rehearsed, everyone attends all the time during the workshop, a rare example of collective concentration.

Writing in 1985, it is hard to remember the different political climate of the early seventies, but the atmosphere of the times certainly informed the work on *Fanshen*. In 1972 and 1974 there had been successful miners' strikes; Jimmy Reid had led the shipworkers on the Upper Clyde to partial victory; workers in the Triumph factory had occupied their factory; there was much talk of workers' co-operatives; anti-Vietnam war protests continued; students frequently tried to gain more control over their own courses. Ideas of participation and control were much debated. In 1974, I was a student. It was still a time of optimism and activism and one of the books currently popular amongst many students was *Fanshen* by William Hinton. At some point I gave or recommended the book to Bill Gaskill. Later that year I was invited to take part in the workshop that was to be part of the process of turning *Fanshen* into a play. I was both excited and curious because I could hardly imagine how the wealth of concrete and painstaking detail about conditions, land reform and political meetings in China in the 1940s was going to turn into a theatrical piece. But there we all were, in St Gabriel's Church Hall, a group of well-fed western actors, trying to come to grips with what it was like to be a Chinese peasant, often close to starvation, who had taken part in the most massive revolution of the twentieth century.

Although we had all read the book, we were still hugely ignorant about Chinese life, politics and culture. Part of the early days of the workshop was taken up with each actor researching a certain area and then giving the others a lecture on it so that we pooled a great deal of information. Paul Freeman told us about the cultivation of certain crops. I had to find out about various household objects such as the *k'ang* (a kind of oven/stove/bed). Di Seymour, who was eventually to design the production, came and talked to us about her visit to China and showed us pictures. Someone came in to teach us the delicately balanced and fluid movements of T'ai Chi and from then on the mornings began with T'ai Chi rather than the normal rumbustious actors' warm-up. At the same time we began tentative improvisations about landlords and peasants under the careful and exciting direction of Max Stafford-Clark and Bill Gaskill. In one of these improvisations we had to greet each other with the words: 'Have you eaten today?' which was the standard form of greeting in certain areas of near-famine. We did this for most of the morning and then rushed off to the greasy café down the road for a huge pile of grub before returning to more similar work. We did improvisations where each member of the company would have to make a speech denouncing something he hated; improvisations where someone would have to persuade the others of the values of Marxism. And we had many discussions. One of the ideas that we adopted from the book and gradually absorbed into our way of working was the notion of discussing everything through until it was resolved to everyone's satisfaction without taking votes. This idea remains to some extent in the structure of Joint Stock itself and the way meetings are conducted.

One of the exercises we undertook during the workshop led us into an area rarely explored by English actors. In the book, land and goods were redistributed after the revolution and in order that they be redistributed equitably, everyone had to be classified either as a rich peasant, a middle peasant or a poor peasant. We decided that in order to understand the process more thoroughly we would classify ourselves. So one afternoon we sat down and everyone in turn talked about their own class background; how much money they had ever earned; what they had in the bank and so on. Needless to say this was utterly fascinating to all of us. Roderic Leigh revealed that although he didn't have much at the time, he was expecting to inherit a fair amount. I think we were all fairly honest about it. And it was an example of the beginning of a way of working that I had never come across in English theatre before, where instead of concentrating solely on character, individual motivation and so forth, we would undertake some sort of class analysis and look at the work from a political perspective. Later this method was to lead to a crisis for Toby Salaman who did not want to relinquish the more traditional method of approaching his part and who eventually left the company.

The rehearsal period was a rare fusion of the political and the aesthetic. Bill

Gaskill and Max Stafford-Clark worked with us on different scenes at different ends of the hall and sometimes with all of us working together. During the workshop we had done one exercise where we formed tableaux taken from a book that Di Seymour had, showing sculptures of pre-revolutionary life. These found their way into the production. One crucial development that came about during rehearsals was the decision to look at each scene in order to discover what the political point of that scene was and how best to make it clear. This, in fact, was an extremely unusual if not revolutionary step for an English theatre company to take. It affected the style of acting that was to develop. Questions about whether we were going to paint our faces yellow, or whether the women should have bound feet or whether we should use cellotape to make our eyes slant more, gradually ceased to be asked as we grappled with ways of making the political ideas clear. This was when Toby left the company. It came to a crunch one day when he was saying – the actor's traditional cry – 'But my character wouldn't do that. He wouldn't behave like that.' But we were no longer at the point where that was the most relevant question to ask and, unable to come to terms with the way the production was going, he left.

There is no doubt that the ideas in the book were affecting and being deeply integrated into our method of work. We began to have self-criticism sessions. At the end of each week we would gather together and criticise the week's work and criticise ourselves too.

During the workshop we had many discussions on design. Someone had imagined it being done in a great mud bowl; someone else had suggested that we perform on a structure of trestle tables with the audience below us. The final design was beautiful and simple. We were, as far as possible, to use authentic props. In the scene of the redistribution of goods, the character I was playing was to receive a cooking pot. As rehearsals drew to a close, I was still unhappy with the one I had been given. I shot off down Lupus Street and, in a junk shop, I found a wonderful, old, cast-iron cooking pot. Just perfect. That was the one I used.

Fanshen had not long opened at the ICA. One night I was getting ready to leave for the theatre and I switched on the telly to catch the news before I left. Vietnam had been liberated. The Vietcong were rolling into Saigon in their tanks. Americans were scuttling for the last helicopters. The show that evening had extraordinary resonance. It seemed more than likely that many of the processes that we were revealing in the play were about to start taking place in Vietnam as they had in China.

Caryl Churchill (writer)

I'd been struck long before by the Ranters and recently thinking about Utopian communities, but none of that was in my mind when Max asked if I'd like to do a show about the Crusades. He had stayed at a house in the country where there was a crusader's tomb and had wondered what would make someone uproot himself and set off for Jerusalem. He suggested Colin Bennett and I write the play together. The three of us met often at Max's flat to share what we had read. We were excited by the ideas but the crusaders themselves remained a bit remote, and when I read Cohn's *Pursuit of the*

Millenium with its appendix of Ranter writings I was seized with enthusiasm for changing to the seventeenth century. We kept the millenial dream and Max's question of why you would turn your life upside down for it, but instead of glimpsing shadowy figures in armour we could hear vivid voices: 'Give give give give up, give up your houses, horses, goods, gold . . . have all things common.'

So there was a new direction for insatiable reading. It leaps at me from a dense notebook, Hill of course, Morton on the Ranters, and pages and pages of quotations from the time. Only a couple of lines about what we did each day at the workshop, but enough to remind me of things I'd forgotten. We were in a church hall near the Old Vic, it was May, it was sunny. It was a large, loose workshop with some actors only dropping in for short visits. We had to learn about something remote and then find how we related to it, so a lot of reading history and then finding equivalents – when did it seem to you that anything was possible? The revolutionary hopes of the late sixties and early seventies were near enough that we could still share them, but we could relate too to the disillusion of the restoration and the idea of a revolution that hadn't happened. (Odd that this was only a year after *Fanshen*; it seemed long after.)

So there was reading and a wallchart; talking about ourselves; and all kinds of things mainly thought up by Max. I'd never seen an exercise or improvisation before and was as thrilled as a child at a pantomime. Each actor had to draw from a lucky dip of bible texts and get up at once and preach, urging some extraordinary course of action justified from the Bible: 'Suffer little children to come unto me' became an impassioned plea to lay children in the street and run them over with a steamroller. They drew cards, one of which meant you were eccentric to the power of that number, and then improvised a public place – a department store, a doctor's waiting room – till it gradually became clear who it was, how they were breaking conventions, how the others reacted. A word in the notebook conjures up half a day's work: 'Songs' – Colin Sell teaching the actors to sing psalms; 'Dives and Lazarus' – we tried acting out parables; 'vagrants' – the actors went out and observed tramps in the street and brought back what they had seen. Already on the third day I find, 'Talked to M – possibly quaker meeting as setting?' and that idea stayed after the workshop. One day we had a prayer meeting where everyone had to speak; someone wanted to eat an apple but Max made him pass it round and everyone had to say something about it; the last person didn't say anything but bit into it; and that ended up in the play. I condensed the Putney Debates so we could read them, and eventually, far shorter again, they went into the play. In a folder I find a scenario I wrote for a day's work: a character for each actor with a speech from before the war, a summary of what happened to them and what their attitude should be at an improvised prayer meeting, and how they ended up at the restoration. This before-during-after idea was something I took forward into the writing. There were improvisations about real people too, Coppe, Clarkson and the Man Who Ate Grass.

Next, the nine-week writing time. Looking at the forgotten notebooks I can catch for a moment the excitement of being so crammed with ideas and seizing on structure, characters, incidents that might contain them. Colin and I were working fairly separately, though agreed on a before-during-after shape, with occasional consultations, and meetings with Max. Two weeks in there is the note, 'C has left'. I establish six characters and a line through for each of them – only one is clearly recognisable, in the final play, as Briggs: 'Poor man, Norman yoke, Leveller. Breakdown, eats grass.' I work out a rather formal structure with many scenes, a meeting in the middle, but what I write not long after is a play consisting almost entirely of one long meeting. Max not surprisingly said it was too static so I scrapped it and started again, intending this time to write a lot of short scenes showing how each character comes to be at the meeting. I played Dylan's 'Lily Rosemary and the Jack of Hearts' again and again to work up a sense of speed and quick story telling. There next seems to be a version close to the final one, though John Evelyn appeared from time to time, reading about scientific advance from his diary. The play was incomplete when rehearsals started, in that not every one of the six characters had a full enough story, but it was enough to start working on.

Now another church hall near Lisson Grove. Only three of the actors from the workshop went on into the rehearsal, so the first part was like another workshop, making the history real again. The main characters were cast and the idea was that everyone would play minor parts in each other's stories. Then Max and I had the idea, first a joke, then seriously, that perhaps there wasn't any need to write the missing scenes if it wasn't quite clear which character was which and different actors played the same character in different scenes. This solved the problem that the extra material would make the play too bulky and plodding (as well as saving me writing it) and also gave an effect we liked of many people having the same experiences during the revolution. We wondered if the actors would mind giving up parts they had been given but they were quite cheerful, keeping their characters for the meeting and swapping them round for other scenes. I did do some writing during the rehearsal. The new structure meant I could add scenes that weren't part of anyone's story, like the butcher. We went to Max's uncle's farm in Buckinghamshire and read the Putney Debates in the farmyard; the actors were sent in to explore the house without anyone in the house knowing they were coming and one of them described being startled by seeing herself in a mirror: that led me to write the scene where one woman gets another to look at herself in the piece of mirror she has looted from the great house. I wrote the description of a battle and Claxton going over the hill after improvisations by Nigel and Will, the first time I'd known the pleasure of giving an actor back a speech in that way, and the only time I remember working quite like that. There was a scene I could never get right despite rewrites and improvisations, a girl tied up to be bled by a doctor, from Hoskins' early life, which ended up, cut very short, in *Vinegar Tom*.

It was August by now, very hot. Did the church hall really have no windows? It had chairs, and Max staged the scenes with these, and that became the set. Sue Plummer designed a beautiful table of scientific instruments and a skull for Evelyn, and then we cut Evelyn. But we kept the table because we liked it so much. Meanwhile Colin Sell was back and the actors were singing the psalms and the Whitman. Sue brought the dark ragged costumes. Steve Whitson came to talk about the lights. The writing was virtually over and the main work now being done by the rest of the company. There were small alterations though up to the opening. All six characters originally had longer speeches at the end, and I think it was at the dress rehearsal at the Traverse that I cut them all down except for Nigel's Man Who Ate Grass. Max and I share a pleasure in making cuts: 'Look, look, we can go from here to here, it still makes sense.' So there we were in Edinburgh, a solemn, tired, silent company. I remember someone saying he'd been surprised the show was so good having seen us looking so miserable. I don't think we were, even then. This is a slight account of a great deal, and one thing it can't show enough is my intense pleasure in it all.

Tony Bicât (writer)

David Hare rang me at the BBC where I was directing my musical *Glitter*.

David: 'I have to do a show with Joint Stock next year. I don't want to write it, would you write it?'

Tony: 'Why me?'

David: 'Well, despite your admittedly damaging early experiences with the theatre, it was good working with you and Nick on *Teeth 'n' Smiles*. Besides I owe you one.'

(A reference to the fact that I had midwifed and co-directed David's first play *How Brophy Made Good*.)

Tony: 'I don't think I'd be very good at writing plays.'

David (ignoring this): 'I thought a show based on *Timon of Athens* . . . Tony are you still there . . .'

Tony: 'What about Bill and Max?'

David: 'What about them?'

Tony: 'To put it mildly, neither of them is a fan of my work.'

David: 'Just read *Timon of Athens*.'

Tony: 'OK.'

David (acid): 'I really appreciate your enthusiasm for this project.'

Two years before, I had seen Peter Brook's *Timon* in Paris, and my reading of the play was coloured by my memory of that production. In Jean-Claude Carriere's superb French version of the text, the play had seemed, despite its exotic cast, very immediate. I sent David a very bald synopsis of the plot, which began 'Timon, a rich Greek . . .'

David: 'Put like this it isn't very encouraging.'

Tony: 'I think wealth is very difficult to stage. For the Elizabethans it was easy, bags of gold. But money now is not gold, but almost an abstract, figures on a computer, things you can't see or touch.'

David: 'I've gone off the idea. Whatever we did, it wouldn't have been as good as Shakespeare.'

Tony: 'Can't we remove the safety net? Do an original play. Start from scratch.'

David: 'You'd be very exposed as a writer in that situation. With no source material to appeal to . . . Believe me I know . . .'

Tony: 'What have I got to lose?'

David: 'Is there something you want to write a play about?'

Tony: 'Well I had the germ of an idea. Supposing there was a prison island, where all the people a future society in England had no use for, were sent. This would give you an interesting group of people to write about . . .'

David: 'Could you get something down on paper by next week?'
Tony: 'I should think so.'
David: 'What about a working title?'
Tony: 'How about "Devil's Island"?'

My plot, which in any case was suspiciously like Howard Brenton's *The Churchill Play*, was speedily abandoned.

I began, as I always do, with people. I start with people I wish to spend some time with, who I in some sense love. Unlike most of my contemporaries, I have never written anything because I read a book or a newspaper article. On my Devil's Island were a Psychiatrist, A Mother, An Hostess, A Businessman, An Immigrant and A Poet. The six characters evolved historically through three times zones, 1937, 1977 and 1997, not ageing but mutating. For example, The Poet became a businessman in 1977 and a wordless clown in 1997.

David: 'I thought you wanted to write about the future.'
Tony: 'I do. But when you sit down to write about the future somehow you always start by looking back.'
David: 'Why?'
Tony: 'It's a springboard.'
David: 'Why do you want to write about the future?'
Tony: 'Because I have children.'
David: 'So have I.'
Tony: 'But I am an optimist.'
David: 'Your notes for Act 3 are decidedly pessimistic . . . bleak.'
Tony: 'It's meant to be comedy.'
David: 'Oh God.'
Tony: 'A cross between J.G. Ballard and *Carry On Up the Khyber*.'
David: 'Ring the Labour Exchange, get me another writer.'
Tony: 'What about the cast?'
David: 'Well Sid James is unavailable so we'll have to make do with Simon Callow.'
Tony: 'Who's Simon Callow?'
David: 'Haven't you seen Snoo's play – *Soul of the White Ant*?'
Tony: 'Not yet . . . I've been writing . . .'
David: 'Then there's . . .'

David gathers a wonderfully heterogeneous and heterodox cast for the Read Through.

David: I think what we are trying to do here, is hijack the writer. Interfere at a stage in the creative process, before it has become fixed. This draft is a stage in the writing that no actors and few directors ever see, essentially a rough first draft. The writer is very exposed, very vulnerable, I therefore urge you to be merciless.'

We early on decided that the writer should write, the actors act and the director direct. But within this conventional set-up, each member of the company was free to stage a morning's work, if they didn't like the way things were going. At some time during the three weeks everybody did this and the discussions from these mornings were very valuable. This apparent democracy however has to be seen in the context of the fact that David and I met an hour before each rehearsal and stayed an hour after to discuss the day's work. This meant that our conflicts for the most part were private, we generally presented a united front and to a certain extent manipulated the workshop to our own ends.

Reading the before-workshop text and the final text now, what surprises me, in view of the three notebooks I have stuffed with notes, is how little the drift of the play changed.

Act 1 is virtually the same, Act 2, although the plot is changed, has very much the same intention. It is only in Act 3 where what I finally wrote bears no relationship to what I originally wrote or any of the futures we improvised. So what did the workshop do to my play?

The short answer is that it made it better.

I tried to start with as few preconceptions as possible. Three time zones, three women, three men. I tried to give the workshop, in return for what it gave me by staging my ideas and scenes, six good strong characters, on the most basic level, good parts to play. I think this is one of the great strengths of the workshop method. You cannot short-change your actors by giving them lousy parts to play. Joint Stock plays are always full of good parts. But at a certain stage, after the workshop, you must take the material back and take it a stage further. It is all too easy to reproduce those wonderful improvisations – a fault with some Joint Stock productions I think.

The workshop made the play better but they did not write it. I wrote it and its failure as a play has to be in the end laid at my door. The Joint Stock method is seductive. It allows you to share some of the burdens of writing – some of the loneliness, but it can also distract you. You can end up wanting to please the workshop too much. In the end the writer in the theatre has power without responsibility. He can create a vision but others – the actors and directors must demonstrate that vision. The writer's task is not to make things easy for the company but to a large extent to make them difficult. So that the ingenuity of actors and directors, which is so much greater than they realise, may rise to unexpected heights. The theatre can do anything. So often it seems to me, it is made to do what it can do easily.

David said that my trouble was I wrote for the theatre as I would like it to be – not as it is. I hope I do.

Devil's Island was a fine production. The acting, as always with David, was faultless. The show was well-designed and lit but after a successful tour, it played to small and dwindling audiences at the Court.

The reviews mirrored the public bafflement. What kind of play was it? Was it a Joint Stock play? No. Was it a Hare–Brenton–Wilson play? No. By all these measures, if measures they were, it fell short. Others became increasingly hysterical in their search for models; names like John Whiting, Tolstoy and Shaw were flung around. Nobody thought that it might be the first play by Tony Bicât, the first Joint Stock play with decent parts for women, the first Joint Stock play that sprung from an original imaginative idea. Although at times I felt a bit like the infantryman who volunteers to lie on the barbed wire while the rest of the platoon charges off to victory, I enjoyed the experience of doing *Devil's Island* and would not have missed it.

The Shortest Joint Stock meeting

Dressing Room 4, Sherman Theatre, Cardiff. 12 January 12.30 p.m.
Present: Complete *Devil's Island* company and Graham Cowley.
Purpose of Meeting: CRISIS.
   Graham: 'The first show at the Roundhouse falls in this financial year and
        we'll need £5,000 to get cracking on the seating. What are we
        going to do?'
Various panic measures suggested – cut *Thought In Three Parts*; borrow; beg;
bank loan etc.
   David: 'Cheat it forward into the next financial year. I'll show you how
        to do it.'
Panic over. Meeting closes 12.47 p.m.

(Company Minutes)

Simon Callow (actor)

For *Devil's Island* Hare had got together a feisty group, including a number
of romantic individualists, a Marxist, an anarchist and an Est graduate. Bicât
was present at all the rehearsals, suggesting exercises and writing down
whatever we produced. He then went away, as we all did. Some of us
languished unemployed (a snag of the Joint Stock method). Others went on a
European tour of the revived *Speakers*.
   We were booked for a midnight spot at the Abbey, as part of the Dublin
Festival. That means that most of the audience had been drinking since 11 a.m.,
just for a start. We, however, were caught up in the cross-currents of
something much bigger. We had decided to do the show with the iron safety
curtain down and the audience on stage with us, our great scaffolding lighting
tower slap in the centre. So at ten past twelve, we started. Immediately we
were heckled as we had never been heckled before: filibustering was more like
it. Eventually, when it was impossible to continue or engage the hecklers in
any kind of dialogue, I said to one of them, as my lower-middle class Socialist
Party of Great Britain speaker, 'OK, mate, you seem to have a lot to say for
yourself, why don't you come up 'ere and tell us all about it'. He clambered
up onto the box, opened his mouth, was unable to orate, so said, 'Oh fuck off
the lot of youse, you're all a load of cunts'. Ironic applause, and I was able to
continue. The speaker to my left had hit on the same ploy. His heckler,
however, similarly silenced by standing on the box, unzipped his fly and
started to urinate on the stage. Mild cries of 'shame' and much mirth.
Suddenly, there was an irruption on the other side of the audience. 'That's the
bastard that killed Frank Stagg!' A tiny white-haired gentleman was suddenly
surrounded by a posse of tough-looking men, all from the audience. It was
Mr O'Dalaigh, the President of the Republic, on an incognito visit, and the
posse were his bodyguard. Swiftly, he was removed from the theatre. His
acusers, who seemed to be connected with our filibusters, were jostled
by remnants of the bodyguard, to cries of 'Shame, let them alone you pigs'
and so on.
   Theatre in Dublin has to put up with a lot of stiff competition from life.
We speakers were valiantly droning on through all this. At last the moment

came for the switch from public to private scenes. The lights change, and the focus is on Van Dyn, the tattooed speaker and his thirteen-year-old helpmate. These scenes, which had commanded rapt attention all over Europe, the audience climbing over each other to be closer to the actors, peering over our shoulders and looking into our nostrils, were actually *heckled* by the Dublin audience, or that element of it clearly bent on disrupting the performance. We ploughed on. Then they hit on a new ploy. In the dark portion of the stage, three men climbed up onto the lighting tower and started swaying it back and forward. If it collapsed, which it was in grave danger of doing, it could easily kill people, not to mention the conflagration that would immediately ensue. The theatre manager was popping about, looking desperately anxious. He beckoned to me. I was the Equity deputy. 'What do you think we should do?' I wasn't sure. I thought that if we could contain the situation we should continue. I hadn't been able to speak to all the actors. I knew that some of them, like me, were frightened by the ugliness of the mood in the audience, but others were angry and defiant. The men had been dragged off the tower, which was now stable, but the uproar, which showed no signs of abating, was impossible to act through. One could hear bottles being broken, and the snarls of angry men. I leapt onto a box and screamed for silence which, unaccountably, fell. 'We are workers,' I said, improbably. 'Like any other workers –.' I suppose I thought the disrupters were the Red Brigade or some Irish equivalent – 'we must have proper working conditions. We're not getting them. If you want us to continue, you must give us a fair hearing. It's up to you.' Total silence. I stepped down. The moment my shoe touched the ground, all hell broke loose. We left the stage. The manager came to see us in the dressing-room. 'Of course, there's no question of the show carrying on. But some of the audience are asking if you'll talk to them, and explain your decision.' We did, and there followed a most extraordinary discussion. On the way to the stage, I said to the Abbey's Artistic Director, the enchanting Tomás McAnna, 'Sorry about all this.' 'Oh don't worry,' he exclaimed, 'this is the Abbey. We're used to riots here.'

The audience, now sitting in the stalls, were certainly in combative mood. There was no hint of an apology, nor much sympathy. Clearly the stage was regarded as a gladiatorial arena. If you didn't like the heat, you should stay out of the kitchen. Their underlying assumption about the relationship of the audience to the actors seemed to be that a state of suspended hostility was the norm, and that by varying the rules and inviting participation we must expect aggression. They were particularly adamant that you couldn't only vary *some* of the rules: one couldn't say 'Participate in some scenes, but not in others'. I could see the force of that, though it had never bothered anyone else in any other part of the world. They had seemed to regard theatre as a game, and what fun it was to be allowed to join in, from time to time. But Dublin clearly regarded theatre as a form of unarmed combat, in which only the fittest survived.

(Edited extract from *Being An Actor*, Methuen London, 1984)

Joint Stock in Europe

Here is the British Embassy, Belgrade.

Joint Stock Theatre Group have props, lighting, etc., in van which broke down in Munich. This needed immediately for International Theatre Festival in Belgrade but Avis not provide new vehicle without 1500DM deposit. Driver also needs petrol money.

HM Ambassador Belgrade would be grateful if you would advance up to maximum 2500DM to driver, on his personal guarantee. Theatre group will be in Germany next week and will arrange repayment.

Is anyone there please?

(Diplomatic telex, September 1976)

Stephanie Fayerman (actress)

A clear cold winter's day in London, January 1977. A room at the top of the Tower Theatre, Islington. The company of Wallace Shawn's *A Thought In Three Parts* recline in pools of white sunlight, around a sweetly singing gas fire.

The mood is expansive as we reflect on the past two weeks spent goose-bumped in bleak basements, hopelessly un-American in this profoundly American piece. In defiance of the elements, we've so far managed to get down to vest-and-knicker acting, but we sense that today is 'get 'em off' day. As Max steps forward, every face struggles to arrange itself into an appropriate expression of gravity. 'Okay, I want each one of you to take us on a magical mystery tour of your body.' His voice is at once paternal and twinkling. 'Tell us the whole story, the bits you're proud of, the bits you would change if you could. And we'll start with Steph.'

Heart pumping, I stand up, but all I can read in the eyes levelled on me is curiosity, amusement, support. 'Okay, so. I'll start at the top. My hair. I love my hair because it's curly and . . .' And so on, down to, to . . . don't stop, just do it. You love your body, not because it would win prizes, but because it has already given you countless hours of pleasure, because it is easy to live in, it is anarchic and cheerful, and a comfort when you're lonely. '. . . and I love that curve like an Irish harp that goes down to – well, I'll show you.' Now it's just the socks and in a rush I realise why I am not ashamed, why it's me here doing this sexually explicit play, and not some other actress. There is nothing to fear, for there is nothing to hide. The feeling is a combination of innocence and power, and I love it.

I sit down and it's the next one right in here please. Neither Tony Rohr nor Philip Sayer will be required to strip during any of the plays, but for the purposes of democracy, today everybody does. Max is next. Lean and cordy, with a back that goes on for days. And then there is Abigail McKern. She flips off her Biba bra and there they are. In the hush that follows, Robyn Goodman leans to me and mutters, 'Shall we leave now?' All stripped, we set about the exploration of each other's bodies. Quite spontaneously, the genders divide and congregate in separate corners. The men earnestly discuss the benefits or otherwise of circumcision, while Paul-John Geoffrey strokes Jack Klaff's hairiness with something approaching awe. The women, meanwhile, are absorbed in the merits and demerits of the large breast and 'to shave or not to shave'.

It soon becomes apparent that, as well as having to resolve the delicate problem of how to mask the simulated sex scenes, there is also a slight matter of age. All the *Youth Hostel* characters are, by definition, youths, and as the next time any of us will see twenty-one again is on somebody's front door, radical measures are called for. In a flash of genius, Robyn suggests white bobby sox. Socks are procured and we instantly shed ten years apiece.

February. The snow lies thick upon the glass roof of the ICA, and Jack is having serious problems with the cold. Having shrunk to an acorn, he first experiments with Deep Heat, but Robyn gags on the pungent fumes every time she has to 'go down' on him, and her subsequent mutinous mutterings leave Jack no choice but to desist. He finally settles for an ingenius little device known (so I am informed) as a 'goat's beard', which enables him to keep his pecker up and thus avoid acute embarrassment and real pain.

Meanwhile, we have opened to near-hysteria from the critics. This play 'is as likely to give offence as anything I have ever seen in the theatre', sniffs the *Telegraph*; the *Standard* critic assures us 'I will not name them (the actors) because their parents might come along and spank them.' As predictably, the *International Times* urges its 'brother hairy apes' (sister apes must presumably stay home in the tree-house and play with their own) to 'see the most relevant apes, see the most relevant play that's on, and defend it.' Despite the *Observer* saying, this is 'maybe the first real sex-farce to reach the British stage', when the reverberations reach their most noble Lordships in the House, it begins to look as if we might *need* defending.

While Lord Donaldson of Kingsbridge, giving a courageous if somewhat lack-lustre performance, attempts to qualify 'the importance of protecting artistic activity from censorship', and Lord Nugent of Guildford asks whether his colleague 'is aware that this show was castigated by the . . . London newspapers for its extreme obscenity', back at the box office, the queue for returns curls out into the Mall. Members of the bowler hat brigade, having legged it straight from the office, are shuffling nervously from foot to foot in a successful, but ultimately pointless, bid to remain incognito behind a phalanx of *Daily Telegraphs*.

Despite Wally's specific intention that the work should 'be understood as a simple piece in three parts', we are all ruefully aware that it is the middle playlet, *Youth Hostel*, which is the main source of all this damp worsted. First comes *Summer Evening*. The bowlers sit through this with ill-concealed discomfort, not least because, being returns, they are forced to sit on floor cushions at the front. With briefcase, rolled umbrella and bowler perched precariously on locked and aching knees, they look and feel thoroughly foolish. Their patience is rewarded with profits, however, when, within minutes of lights up on the second piece, a teenage couple appear to be going at it with all the mechanical enthusiasm of rabbits. In some of his earlier notes, Wally recommends that 'the sex is acted in a more or less naturalistic way, although the acts don't take as long as they really would.' Within the next 35 minutes, four of us average seven 'orgasms' each, in almost every imaginable combination of gender and activity.

The effect is, at once, hilarious and heart-breaking. As the lights fade, each blanket-clad figure is discovered in shivering isolation, each one a victim of a kind of cultural malnutrition, which leaves them exhausted but unreplete. In the darkness that follows, the only sound is a grunt, thump and occasional fart, as the bowlers haul themselves to their feet and stampede for the exit. . . . In time to miss the ten-minute spoken daydream which is *Mr Frivilous*.

On high-days and Saturdays, the show is a joy to perform. The house is bright and alive with blushing teenagers, whooping friends, and dewy-eyed OAP's who sit holding hands, all dreamy and tender with (one assumes) reminiscences of times past. And backstage afterwards it's 'Hey Steph, how did you get that "come" on your chest?' 'Spit dear, just a little human spit.'

Then it's Monday again and the city sidles in, bringing something with it, something dark, ugly and mean. And having been blithely unselfconscious, suddenly, sitting naked within inches of the nearest buffed black brogue, I waver. I am suddenly conscious of my nakedness and I am furious. God help me, I could be earning three times the money at Paul Raymond's up the hill. But that's not the point. Damn them for making this something less than it is, for making me feel momentarily graceless and grubby. Being a sex object is profoundly depressing and I won't have it. Open the legs a little wider, gross them out!

The characters in *Youth Hostel* crammed their day with every kind of instant sexual gratification in an effort to fill the arid wastes of their spiritual and cultural lives. No wonder those paragons of public decency and order were so incensed all those years ago. They had a nasty suspicion they'd been rumbled.

Max Stafford-Clark (director)

What is Joint Stock? Many meetings and conversations concerned themselves with this question. It became our hardy perennial. When new members of the company opened it up the old hands groaned. The following extracts are from my own notes of company meetings held during 1977, the year of the permanent ensemble.

Friday, 5 March 1977, St Gabriel's Parish Hall Twenty-two people at mammoth policy meeting. Eighteen wear jeans, four do not.

Pip Donaghy: 'We all need to fanshen.' He talks very emotionally and we are all a little embarrassed. 'Joint Stock must fanshen.' I stay looking down and don't want to meet people's eyes.

Simon Callow: 'The personality of Joint Stock has come from the directors. We must appraise that.' But he only offers in exchange that we should 'try to produce theatrical work of a very high quality'.

Gillian Barge: 'Other people can have the bright ideas which I can then support and get my energy from that.'

Howard Brenton: Commends our intense social observation. 'Having watched that policeman bleed all over the floor for three hours (A superintendent from the Met had come to the *Mad World* workshop) the question was asked, can we do him?'

Will Knightley: 'What we tried to do with *Yesterday's News* was to arrive at a consensus without the guidance of a clear political point of view which had been provided for us by the book of *Fanshen*.'

Graham Cowley: 'I think it's my job to like the shows.'

Jane Wood: 'I feel guilty about having a kid in this collective. You can't negate your whole life because you've joined a theatre group.'

Paul Freeman: 'If we were going to have a coherent political point of view it would have emerged by now.'

Barrie Keeffe: 'I think it's important to go from show to show and not be too concerned about our public image . . . The real change is from verbal work to spectacular shows.'

Paul Freeman: 'What Bill and Simon both feel is that we lack a centre . . . a principle that binds us together.'

Bill Gaskill: 'We should be developing the work we want to do and putting it in front of the public . . . We must decide who is going to write the plays and who is going to direct them.'

Tom Wilkinson: 'Unless there's some kind of articulated credo the work will founder . . . Who do you wish to address?' Here comes the move towards populism again.

Cecily Hobbs: 'I don't think it's just a question of vulgaring it up.'

Bill Gaskill: Feels that our standard of work has dropped since *Fanshen* and that's because we have lost what we are doing it for, what centre we are operating from.

Tuesday, 9th March 1977, St Gabriel's Parish Hall Thirteen people wearing jeans, one not.

Simon Callow: 'Well here we are again then, staring baffled and bemused into a circle.'

Friday, 14 October 1977, Salisbury Playhouse On tour with *Fanshen*.

'Seeing it again I found it very invigorating', said Bill of *Fanshen*, which he had come down to see last night. 'The Labour Movement has lost its idealism and it's exciting to see a vision of it.'

We discuss our commitment to Joint Stock. Bill is going to direct an opera in Wales. Cecily and I want to stay with Joint Stock. 'That's because you're not being offered any other work', says Paul.

Bill Gaskill: 'There's no reason why we should think Joint Stock is everything'.

Bruce Alexander: 'If you're in the business of taking the temperature of the times you have to go out and test it from time to time.'

How? Not by doing other theatre jobs and not by being out of work.

Definition of socialism discussed.

Will Knightley: 'Yes, but you have to start by talking about your own social vision and what you feel socialism should be . . . Most of our relationships are based on feeling threatened and how we cover it up.'

We try to define how we should start to discuss our own beliefs in socialism and in the work we have been doing.

Paul Freeman: Condemns 'loose, trendy socialism'.

David Rintoul: Discusses how we became a collective. Paul is attacked for his definition.

The question is defined as 'Why I joined the collective'. Everybody answers.

Paul Freeman: 'Progression . . . Ideas of *Fanshen* . . . Opportunities to control my own work . . .' Relates how he enjoyed 'struggle with management' before Joint Stock became a collective.

The ink changes colour here because I'm asked to stop taking notes as Cecily feels threatened. My writing gets smaller and I keep taking notes.

Discussion is endless and circular. What is socialism? Are we a socialist theatre group? Can we make decisions about what work we are to do for the year? How do we put socialist theory into practice via Joint Stock?

But true harmony at last: all fourteen of us are wearing jeans.

Tony Rohr (actor)

I was a busker, a bookie, a trainer and the race course in *Epsom Downs* – the last in a green suit with a piece of artificial grass in my hand, smoking a cigarette in a long elegant holder. I also played a horse. I knew a lot about horses. When the company spent a day at the Derby I backed the winner at 6 to 1 – Lester Piggot on The Minstrel. Playing a horse was not quite so easy. At an early rehearsal, Howard Brenton insisted the actors cast as horses should be naked. Not stripped to the waist, or wearing a jockstrap but completely starkers. 'A horse is a naked animal', he said, trying to sound reasonable. Bill thought it a wonderful theatrical image. (Max was directing the show.) When it came to the photo call the press were asked not to use any full length shots of the scenes with the horses. We didn't want the wrong kind of publicity or to ruin the moment in the show. This was Joint Stock after all. As soon as I appeared in my leather harness, the cameras clicked, the tabloids shuffled towards the stage. But, as good as their word, all the photos that appeared in the papers after the first night were cut off at the waist. Except, that is, for those that turned up in a little-known French magazine, a copy of which I was sent under plain cover some years later. Inside, between an article entitled 'Les femmes sont-elles excitées par l'idée du viol?' (Answer: 'Oui') and an ad for some kind of equipment, were the horse shots from Epsom Downs – full length, un-cropped, un-retouched. The text, in French, went as follows:

What beautiful stallions! This appears to be the verdict in London of Howard Brenton's play, directed in a *very* realistic manner by Max Stafford-Clark. As far as we can make out, the play is about horse-racing: the course, the bookies, the lords and ladies who come to stroke the prancing animals, smack their rump, fondle them in the enclosure.

Substitute men for horses and you have the idea. It's certainly something to think about . . .! Mind you, some women we know are already thinking along these lines and treat us men like stallions to be led to the rut. All the same, it takes some cheek to pull it off. It seems that once again London is ahead of us, at least as far as sex is concerned. But how did they cast the show? With an ad saying 'Wanted – Men hung like horses'? What if they were to revive Davy Crockett? Would it be 'Wanted – Men with balls like a bear'? The possibilities are endless. We'll leave you to think of them. Have fun!

As they say, a good notice is a good notice. And this must be Joint Stock's only review in a porno mag. But for my money, the ultimate accolade for an actor playing a horse is a notice in *Sporting Life*. 'EPSOM DOWNS – A GAMBLE THAT PAYS OFF', it began, paying passing attention to the cast's 'gambling fever' before concluding:

Rohr appears in his birthday suit as a horse running in the Derby. He also plays a trainer who bears an uncanny resemblance to Guy Harwood and for me he stole the show.

'I'm a Derby outside chance' hardly sounds a classic line but if you can imagine Rohr, naked but for a harness, trotting round the paddock you will appreciate why it brings roars of laughter.

Simon Callow portrays Les Backshaker as if he's been a bookmaker all his life, while others to star are Paul Freeman, as a racing man who sounds a ringer for Max Wall, and David Rintoul, whose commentary on the Derby might make several professionals blush.

Criticisms are few. Stable lads, though six-footers, acquit themselves admirably, although the one leading Rohr round the paddock looks like a kennel-man dressed in his long khaki coat.

The play is well worth a visit, though with the seats as hard as Epsom in a drought, it may be wise to take a saddle with you.

Max Stafford-Clark (director)

Epsom Downs was a workshop that started with a version of the play already written. Our work had been to scrutinise Howard's script and amend it in the light of our experience. We had talked to Lord Wigg, to someone from Gamblers Anonymous, to a trainer, and to a stable lad. A party had been to Newmarket but on Wednesday 1 July all of us went to the Derby: The Minstrel's Derby. Here is the discussion that took place the next day back in rehearsal.

Thursday 2 June 1977, Riverside Studios

Talking about Derby. General jollity.

Gillian Barge: Amount of alcohol being consumed. Beer bottles everywhere.

Simon Callow: Excuse for jamboree. Components for vacuum cleaners being sold. Not many middle-class people. Chefs hired by works outings. Fellini. Hated frothing steeds. Absolutely working-class celebration.

David Rintoul: Like a medieval encampment early in the morning. Regional differences between bookies. Villains sitting in their yellow Rolls Royce Corniche.

Howard Brenton: Care people had taken. Like an Ealing Studios fifties British film. People screwing legs into tables . . . vast picnics bought. Slowness of the build up. Violence and ecstasy of a football match not there. Different kind of celebration. Gipsies were wonderfully dignified.

Paul Freeman: No idea England had so many bookmakers. Found Queen and whole morning suit thing obnoxious . . . at the end those people had removed themselves by money and class. Crazy divotmen. Small sense of frustration because there was no natural consummation. People stripping their clothes off . . . trying to make a climax that wasn't there.

Jane Wood: British eccentricity . . . the Queen one moment . . . have you had a letter from Jesus the next.

Cecily Hobbs: 'So vulgar', not seventies at all . . . sort of timeless feel about it. Anti-climax because race is over so quickly.

Tony Rohr: Backing the winner. 'Lost my head.' Gypsies were so well off. Beauty of gypsy girls 'hair all beautifully done in ringlets'. Sense of it building up. Once the Derby's over everything petering out. Timeless. Hallucinogenic feeling. Great tables groaning with food. As day went on people got more and more drunk. One man desperately trying to stand up but crashing down again. Zoom in to race and pull out again. Just two minutes. Incredible names of bookies. Barney Goldshaker. Loonies walking the course. Guardsmen. Willie Carson must have had the shits when he couldn't shake Lester off. Milliondollarman nearly won. 'I would have been eating at the Ritz.'

Bob Hamilton: 'Buy a charm off an old gypsy.' She was 12. Took photos of hoods but didn't dare do it directly so Tony and Dave stood in front of them.

Try cutting from scene to scene as quick as possible. From one improvisation to another.

PM. We talk now about the play. I raise difficulties as I see them. How real? Should characters be followed through in second half? How many of these incidents are of interest to Howard?

Cecily Hobbs: Play should say we are happy to see the status quo working.

Simon Callow: Didn't envy people in the enclosure . . . 'trapped up there in their morning suits unable to move.' Wanted play to show how great the power of the crowd was and to swing on that tide. It would be a misrepresentation to show the crowd being manipulated and unhappy because they were having a good time.

Will Knightley: Wanted the play to culminate in short sharp scenes like the vignettes we've been doing.

Jane Wood: Was worried about the blending of documentary and fantasy.

Max Stafford-Clark: Why is Emily going to kill herself? Does her personal oppression concern us? Or does she stand for oppression of women in general?

Tony Rohr: Would like to see the characters in the first half fleshed out and followed through. The character of Emily worries him because she has no muscle. What is it that Howard wants to show?

David Rintoul: What is it that we want to show and how? About Derby . . . about class today?

Howard Brenton: 'It's a play about the class struggle . . . even if Derby Day itself is half-time in that struggle.' Emily has to be blown up out of proportion because she's the only plot. Fact or fiction? It's got to be fact. 'It's got to be epic because you are picking the leaves out of the ocean. Each scene has got to make a point.'

Simon Callow: 'How can it be a swindle? I'd like to push you on that.'

Howard Brenton: 'I would like them to own the horses.'

The conversation begins to fragment and it comes down to Simon Callow and Gillian against the rest of us. 'I get tired I suppose of being always on the right side,' says Gillian.

Howard Brenton: Uses his great violent metaphors. He says he wants to scrap the play so far and use it as lumber with which to reconstruct. The play has been smashed against the reality of the event.

It's true that it's no good simply witnessing events . . . however accurately we can do it . . . there also has to be some analysis . . . but it's also true that there's a general nastiness in Howard's play that we simply didn't see yesterday. There were no policemen beating up tramps . . . no mothers abandoning their babies, no pockets picked . . . but it's difficult to write a vibrant play about people having a good time.

Hayden Griffin comes in and says he doesn't want to work with me and says he needs someone with Bill's experience to do it. 'Max is not a director I feel a particular sympathy with . . . it needs a director who has experience of working on a large scale.' Company rally round and confidence expressed by all. Hayden offers advice on other designers. This is rejected. He leaves.
Howard Brenton prefers the idea of Peter Hartwell. 'He would be better than one of the burnt-out heavies.'
Paul Freeman: 'Nobody is indispensable except possibly you' (to HB).
Howard Brenton: 'Only indispensable people are the actors.'
   We make a list of groups of people we saw at the Derby who we haven't got in the play. These include: hamburger sellers; works outings; religious fanatics; heavy drinkers; hawkers; vendors; mental deficients; tipsters. Howard writes as fast as he can: 'I'm getting Parkinson's Disease. I'm so furious.'
   Exercise for tomorrow: whole group in works outing. Exercise is simply to cross the stage and we should be able to tell what time of Derby Day it is.
   And so to bed.
   A lively day.

Alison Ritchie (stage manager)

One night during the interval of *Epsom Downs*, an anxious-looking woman came up to me and said, 'Excuse me. I think the theatre's on fire.' For a stage manager this is like being told you've landed *Hamlet* at the National – a rare moment of excitement tinged with disbelief. I followed her gaze and saw a tiny plume of smoke billowing from the lighting rig. Stage managers are supposed to stay calm in the face of a crisis, whether it's the sudden disappearance of a pair of trousers about to feature in a twenty-second costume change or, as in this case, the prospect of the theatre burning down. Reassured by the sight of a technician racing backstage silently mouthing what looked like 'fire' I told the woman to sit down and not worry. While the audience did their bit for the Roundhouse bar, we did ours for the roof.
   I first worked for Joint Stock on *Light Shining in Buckinghamshire*, after a two-year spell in rep. I answered an ad in the *Stage*, met Max – who I'd never heard of – and soon found myself working in the grottiest rehearsal room I've ever seen in my life. A Labour Party branch would have suspended standing orders and decamped to the local pub. We stayed. Technically, the show was very simple – six chairs, a table, a shelf and a tarpaulin – so it was easily adapted to the different spaces on tour. Life on the road, however, turned out to be pretty dreary, mainly because the actors wanted to sleep all the time. I'd heard it said you could recognise Joint Stock actors by the bags under their eyes and imagined late nights in local clubs, afternoon excursions to see the sights. Instead, the hardest part of the tour was persuading the

actors to get out of bed. Feeble lot.

Happily, this proved to be untypical of Joint Stock tours. As the company moved into its collective phase – I made endless cups of tea during the transition – the energy and inventiveness of the work on stage was soon matched off the boards. The actors took to living on a barge, wherever possible travelling to the venue by canal. This was not without its hazards. Gillian Barge fell into a canal, the boat sank when it was caught on a lock gate and during the *Fanshen* revival the car used to bring the actors to the theatre broke down. A packed house in Mold saw the lights go up on some rather breathless Chinese peasants.

After *Light Shining*, the design work got more ambitious. *Devil's Island* had a large rostrum with various floorings and we graduated from a transit to a Luton van for the tour. *Mad World* had a wooden floor that led to a dispute between Bill and Hayden Griffin, the designer. It was scheduled to be painted yellow gloss but Bill decided he preferred the plain wood. Hayden thought the wood 'arty', Bill said the yellow made him feel sick. Hayden won and to my mind the comedy took off from that point. Little did I know I was destined to spend hours getting paint off the costumes. It looked good but it took weeks to dry.

As might be expected, paint posed a few problems on *The Ragged Trousered Philanthropists* – there was a lot of it around. Without doubt, this was the hardest show I worked on but it was also the most rewarding. One problem was how to clean the flats so expertly painted during the first act. The original idea was to use 'washable' paint and the actors agreed to do wash duty every day before the show. We tried it and each flat took two hours of hard scrubbing. In the end, Peter Hartwell, the designer, taught the actors to break down the paint with sprays and white spirit which was much more fun. This proved the best solution, though after the Riverside run we had to strip thirty coats off the flats just to be able to lift them.

There were occasional spillages. Harriet Walter emptied a bucket of white emulsion over a woman's skirt; Danny Boyle, serving his time as an assistant stage manager, earned what is best described as a cool look when he knocked a bucket and delayed the opening in Plymouth by twenty minutes. But the biggest problem was simply the size of the show. For the first time, we toured a lighting rig to supplement what was available at the venues and Andy Phillips, the lighting designer, came to every gig. One early get-out ended at four o'clock in the morning with the next get-in scheduled to start an hour later in Hull. The whole thing was only made possible because the actors worked on the get-outs, dismantling the set, loading the van with the rest of us. Whatever is said about the collective management of the company, the real pay-off is the commitment everyone brings to the work. I would never have done a show like *Philanthropists* for any other company. Life is too short.

Stephen Lowe (writer)

For *Philanthropists*, we spent a month painting and decorating a disused warehouse in Plymouth. The mornings were devoted to painting, the afternoons to working on the play. Towards the end of the workshop, we improvised the works outing – the annual beano – that forms a central episode in Tressell's novel. As it turned out, the evening was to have a decisive influence on our vision of the play. Bill Gaskill, Peter Hartwell, the designer, the actors and myself were joined by Max Stafford-Clark and two of the builders working on the conversion of the warehouse – Fred the carpenter and Pete the paint. Our hosts were the students and staff of the Theatre Department at Dartington College. The following account is taken from letters I wrote during the workshop.

At lunch we raided Ross's, an ex-army surplus shop, and Oxfam, for old suits, shirts, to wear at the beano, went through the songs again, and the rough order of the scenes, dressed up and waited to be picked up in a van. We each took a character from the book which we were to 'play' for the evening. We were uncertain as to how things would work out at Dartington, in their beautiful dining-hall – all we planned was that we would have the meal, make the speeches and sing the song, and take it from there.

When we arrived, we were met at the main entrance to the Great Hall by an old lady who welcomed us to her hotel. We stood, confused by the splendour, desperately holding on to our hats, then entered the dining-room where four wenches, in white lace aprons, were waiting (these somewhat threw the improvisation for some of us by their sheer beauty). The lady at the door was, it turned out later, the wardrobe mistress; the girls, first-year drama students who had been told no more than to arrive and serve the mad Joint Stock their meal, in period Edwardian.

We sat down to dinner, the men at one end of a long table under the main chimney; Hunter (Chris Burgess) stranded, alone, at the far end. Rushton (Bill Gaskill) was in the middle of a second table, with some students and Grinder (Max Stafford-Clark) who appeared a little later, not in costume. The second table was taken up by college staff.

A barrel of beer had been laid on for the men and Hunter was apparently drinking lemonade which he obtained by slipping the waitress money.

The meal was soup, sausage and tomato pie with leeks and potatoes, and a variety of desserts, jellies, etc. Oddly, characters began to slip from caricature to character (with only the occasional breakout) as the drink had its effect. It was relatively good humoured among the men.

Then Hunter started the speech, and Chris really did look like the description in the book. Crass (Fred Pearson) gave the accounts, and the surplus to be given out among the men was greeted with cheers. Barrington (Mark Wing-Davey) and I (as Owen) stayed out for the 'For he's a jolly good fellow' for Rushton and Grinder, and we both felt extreme disgust, but stayed quiet. Then Grinder made his speech, attacking the socialists, which the men enjoyed, goading us to speak. Suddenly, Barrington rose and began his defence. Slowly, carefully, with the strength of suppressed rage. The evening became electric. Everyone remained silent – perhaps too silent. The defence was clear, powerful. I was deeply moved and, towards the end, was able to look around, with some pride in my beliefs as Owen.

At the end, Crass broke in with 'No more speech-making' and the singing began. He sang the Tory work song 'Work Boys Work . . .' which everyone bar the socialists joined in happily. I was angry with Philpott (Kenny Ireland) and Semi-Drunk (Peter-Hugo Daly), who had expressed some socialist leanings, for not realising what they were doing.

Then Mrs Payne (Harriet Walter) stepped forward to sing 'Who Will Buy My Flowers?', accompanied by Semi-drunk on the piano. This was a sentimental Victorian song which, in rehearsals, we had all done cod crying to, but now there was none of that. The reality of this song moved us all – I felt it was a good description of all our states, and if only we listened, people would change, others were genuinely moved at what before seemed only trite pathos. We joined in the chorus and the harmonies felt beautiful. It was the first moment of real beauty in the evening.

Semi-Drunk tried to sing 'Put Me Among the Girls' and was shouted down (he had in fact started the singing with 'Old Bull and Bush'). Then, accompanied by Barrington on a £3000 violin the college had found, Payne (Bruce Alexander) sang 'Don't Go Out Tonight, Dear Father', a song which no one could take seriously, which went on and on as intended in the book. But it was cod, it was too acted, i.e. a man singing badly and boringly – a dreary song with gestures. Our reactions as a group, instead of being spontaneous and diverse, were calculated and forced. Philpott then sang 'The Roast Beef of Old England', forgetting almost all the words (quite genuinely) much to the amusement of the lads. Crass rounded off with a political comic song, 'Two Lovely Black Eyes' in which we all joined the chorus.

This then was the end of the songs we had rehearsed. According to the book we should now have gone outside to play games, walk round the grounds, etc. Instead, the evening took an unexpected course, led off by the warmth of Fred's personality. After a pause, he suddenly began to sing a Geordie song, in one of the loveliest voices I ever heard. Quietly, individually, others began to sing, moving somewhere along the dividing line between character and their own identity (gradually letting their characters drift away from them, slowly revealing the group as a group of actors). I forget now the songs that were sung, but everything moved quietly, unforced, from one to the next, some funny, some gentle – nothing boisterous, nothing disruptive, no one shouting anyone down. Just the group enjoying and relishing the talents of its fellow members. Ken stood up and did a monologue for the north (as Bill and I could not think of anything) of the little lad who gets ate by the lion. The waitresses sang a first world war song, beautifully, and one of them recited a monologue. Scottish songs were sung, and the hymns we had sung in rehearsal – 'The Living Stream' and 'Work, for the Night is Coming' were sung so beautifully I felt like crying. Peter-Hugo played two of his compositions on the piano. Mark sang two revolutionary modern songs from a musical on Carpenter. Peter Hartwell did a Canadian song. During all this Hunter stayed in character, suddenly leaping up to sing the National Anthem. At first, he was paid lip service to by the men, led by Crass, and tried to sing the first line of a song, demanding that the men joined in. We let him carry on on his own until he could remember no more. He would return to his seat, jump again, stumble out a few demented, drunken words, and collapse back. No one minded. He was ignored, powerless, the men were together. What significance did he have? He was just a sad, black clown. The company accepted him without malice, stripping him of power. It was the most telling image of the night. The pauses in between songs and monologues were silent, reverential, full of warmth. I went to the lav at one point and missed what was apparently another high spot. Pressure had been put on Fred the carpenter to do a number representing the south. He refused, and Peter-Hugo stood up and, quietly, without a trace of cockney, recited a Thomas Hardy poem. Everyone was thunderstruck. This, if possible, was topped by Pete the paint, who suddenly broke into a song about Plymouth and Drake, in a beautiful bass voice, managing about six verses before he forgot it. It didn't matter. We all now were one group.

Eventually, in one last attempt to gain control, Hunter discovered a ball and led us all out into the spreading darkness on the lawn, to play ball games. All characters bar his were now gone. We stood in the beauty of the trees, as he disappeared across the lawn, clutching onto a young waitress, her white half hidden by his black as they faded across the lawn.

We stood around, talking to the college people, the lads' thoughts now turning towards female companionship. I doubt if any of us actually asked any of the 'audience' what they had thought of the evening. It had been a totally selfish act, something specifically for the group for which they had been needed. But I think they enjoyed it. I'm not too worried about that. Pete Hartwell got off with a charming first year drama student, Max prowled around looking for his opportunity. At around eleven, Bill sounded retreat for the Great Return. Chris could not be seen as we piled into the cars and set off home. On the way back, Bruce Alexander and I discussed life, women, marriage – and Pete the painter chatted up Harriet. At home, we discussed with Bill the night's happenings. He is over the moon with it. So am I. How can we use it? Got to sleep around 3.00, but awoke at 5.00 feeling less than well, staggering around the place. Had visions of blood poisoning (of the alcoholic type). Decided to go on the waggon for a bit.

The final sequence to the beano is Chris's story. We all assumed he had made it. However, it transpired that, through an alcoholic haze, he heard the bus moving on, and ran out across the lawn after it. This sad, bowler-hatted figure chasing it down the perfect drive. Unable to catch up, someone told him Pete was still around so he wandered around the college crying out his name, forlornly. Pete, who was tucked up in bed by that time, did not heed the call. Chris finally slept in some student's house, rising at 6.00 for the three mile walk into town to catch the 7.00 to Plymouth. What with his hangover and his strange clothes, the vision of this man slinking through the small town at the crack of dawn is one to conjure with. The bus took one and a half hours to get to Plymouth (a distance of some twenty-five miles) and from there he bolted to the site to get there for nine o'clock. However, when he arrived there no one turned up. We had, in fact, made a call that night for 11.00 at the rehearsal room.

(Edited extract from *Letters from a Workshop*,
Dartington Theatre Papers, 1979)

Danny Boyle (director)

'This is Bill Gaskill.'

For a drama graduate, fresh out of Bangor, landing the assistant stage manager's job on *Philanthropists* was like stowing away on Concorde. No amount of paint swilling dampened the excitement. I'd read about Bill Gaskill in books.

'Actually, Bill's work always catches the critics napping.'

I don't believe it. The actors are scared, that's all. The tour settles it. The carriage chase is brilliantly staged, precarious acrobatics atop what were tables only seconds before. In Hull's Transport and General Workers' Union hall, packed with retired trade unionists, the workers' betrayal by the emerging Labour Party is presented with all the qualities of a good night out. The London run produces a persistent and mysterious fan. High above the evening in the vacant sound box a shadowy figure returns two or three times a week. And each time at the same point of the play. The carriage chase.

Having toured it for months, I could watch Newsnight instead, remember the OAPs stamping their feet in excited recognition, see my dad forgetting this was a theatre, realise the *Guardian*'s second stringer was snoozing off his interval and ask who is the secret figure studying the scene?

'That's Peter Gill.'

Miriam Margolyes (actress)

They needed a lesbian for a play about sexual politics. I auditioned for Max and Caryl on the phone – shouting across the wires from Italy where I was on holiday. I knew Max and Julie Covington and Carole Hayman – none of the others. On the first day of rehearsal Max explained the work process. I was on a high for weeks; it was the rehearsal process for me which means Joint Stock and I remember the 'truth sessions' – sitting in a circle each day, one of us in the middle, telling everything about our lives, our sexuality, and our insecurities – trusting a group of near strangers with buried secrets and private fears. Was it a sort of EST with Equity money? I don't know but the power of such moments will never leave me. The structured improvisations, feeding each others' imaginations, laughter and terror mingling, as we wrestled with Max's witty and malicious comments. It was a spurious democracy – he had the real power but he did try to make us take the responsibility. He forced me to grow up as an actress (which must mean as a person too) and to examine in detail, line by line, my objectives through a scene, an act – the whole play. Lacking a drama school discipline I had never properly worked on preparing a part, and the gaps in my technique were cruelly but necessarily exposed by Max. I remember the 'self-criticism' session, which I had to cancel a lucrative voice-over to attend (Max was very scornful of such earnings) and my inability to find fault with myself but being full of criticism of the others. Max said I was the best *directed* person. I think he might not have meant it as a compliment to me but who cares. The joy of such good work – my moment as the Grandmother trying to murder a doll, Julie's speech as the Mother in Part 2 and Tony Sher as a revolting but accurately observed infant – stuff of which real theatre is made.

Tony Sher (actor)

Back in 1978 I was not familiar with the term 'sexual politics', so I hesitated when Max Stafford-Clark invited me to join a workshop on that theme as the next Joint Stock project. What could it possibly mean? Sex was sex and politics was politics and putting them together surely took the fun out of both.

However, I was easily persuaded by Max, who had recently become my guru as a result of working together on two shows at the Royal Court. He assured me that the meaning of sexual politics was precisely what we would all be seeking to define through the workshop and that, intriguingly, we would be using *ourselves* as research material. The group was being chosen for their versatility not just of talent, but of lifestyle. Thus the collection assembled for the workshop (not all of whom were eventually to be involved in the play) included a straight married couple, a straight divorced couple, a gay male couple, a lesbian, a lesbian-to-be, at least two bisexual men, no bisexual women, and then, of course, the usual large number of heterosexuals – that is, when they weren't dabbling in the other categories. Finally, observing this cross-section, this Noah's Ark of human sexuality, was our playwright Caryl Churchill, herself a committed and tolerant feminist.

One of the first things that became apparent about sexual politics as we commenced the workshop, was that it is essentially concerned with attitudes towards sex rather than the practice thereof, and thus best investigated fully-clothed. This was something of a relief to me because some previous Joint Stock shows had required the actors to run around the stage in the nude either masturbating or pretending to be racehorses, and these were things I generally preferred to do at home.

The atmosphere in our workshop was relatively studious. There were books to be read – predictable titles like *The Female Eunuch* and *With Downcast Gays* – discussions to be had, interviews to be done with any groups not already represented. For example, our average age was thirty to forty so we had no personal experience of older generations to draw upon. This information was to be supplied by the unlikeliest source.

Working as caretaker at the rehearsal rooms was a woman in her mid-fifties, a hard, closed character who had resisted all our gestures of politeness and friendship. Eventually we stopped trying, after every attempt to move a chair from one room to another or to fill the kettle had been met with growled aggression; all of us, that is, with the exception of Julie Covington who is blessed with a nature that constantly seeks out the best in everyone. She persisted with a show of friendship and then one day, much to our surprise, announced that the woman had expressed curiosity about our workshop and Julie had invited her to join one of our sessions. The woman came in with her defences down, puzzled to be receiving friendship after so much animosity and flattered by our interest in her. Soon she was telling us her life story which, not surprisingly, was full of harsh personal relationships: a strict upbringing, a husband who had beaten her, men constantly being dismissive and cruel until recently when she had met one who was different and with whom she had finally, in her middle age, been able to experience her first 'organism'. We asked her what it had felt like and her answer was to inspire the title of our play – 'It was like being on cloud nine.'

Throughout the workshop we each took turns to tell our own life stories and to answer questions on our sexual experiences and lifestyles. It was nerve-wracking to contemplate (and far more revealing than stripping naked would have been) and so it is to the credit of the group that these sessions became the most exhilarating of all. Through them the real meaning of sexual politics was becoming clear. Each of us was secure in our separate territory, male, female, gay, straight, married, single, or whatever; brain-washed by different upbringings and prejudices. However liberal we each previously thought ourselves, we were now face to face with 'the others' and so many preconceptions were proving to be wrong. It would be easy to satirise this part of the workshop as a sixties hippy encounter group, but I think we were experiencing something valuable, exchanging prejudice for knowledge.

There was also a practical side to the workshop, improvisations and acting exercises to illustrate what we were learning. Here Max's 'status games' came into their own. They are practised with a pack of cards numbered two to ten which represent the power of your status. To start with you simply draw a card and then attempt to enter a room or greet someone to the power of that number. A 'two' would be shy and retiring, a 'ten' would be bold and confident. That's relatively easy to master; it becomes trickier when trying to differentiate between say a 'five' and a 'six'. But once the skill has been practised with these basic exercises it can become much more sophisticated. For example, a white, heterosexual, married, successful businessman would probably be regarded as a 'ten' in our present society while a black, lesbian, single mother working as a prostitute might be regarded as a 'two', but in a situation where the man visits the woman and finds himself riddled with guilt and shame while she is comfortably on her own territory just doing her job, each status might fluctuate and eventually they might be completely reversed.

The method became affectionately known as 'acting by numbers', but like many good concepts its simplicity is what is so thrilling. It becomes a common language in discussing human behaviour and, when working on a text, it serves as a useful shorthand between director and actor: 'In that scene you should try playing a "three" rather than a "five".'

Another use Max made of his card games was to illustrate what it is like to be gay in this society. A set of the court cards were returned to the pack and whoever drew these were gay (I'm afraid we did succumb to the temptation of using the Queen for this exercise) and had to seek out one another and make contact in, say, a park or art gallery without arousing the attention of all the other (straight) people there. The danger of this situation would then be increased by the addition of one extra court card, say the Joker, into the shuffle and whoever drew this had to play a policeman on an assignment where he's masquerading as gay in order to catch people soliciting. Now the improvisation was played with the 'Queens' again trying to make contact, but hopefully with one another and not the 'Joker'.

The workshop lasted three weeks and it was a very happy time for us all, with a fabric of trust, honesty and affection being woven between us which the group was never to enjoy again in subsequent rehearsals or the tour. The rot began to set in with the enforced two-month break while the play was being written. This was, in my opinion, the most disastrous part of the Joint Stock structure as it then operated, with the actors left suspended, unpaid but half-committed to the project. The idealism of the workshop was quickly corrupted into a paranoia about what the actual written play and, crucially, the *parts* would be like. There was always the temptation to seek other work which, unless it fitted perfectly, would then make one unavailable for the Joint Stock project when it resumed. From an actor's point of view, I think it was preferable when Joint Stock operated as a permanent company and the gap between workshop and rehearsals could be effortlessly filled with performances of a previously workshopped project. We, however, had been assembled solely for *Cloud Nine* and so the two month gap duly took its toll, both on us (with the group chemistry mysteriously evaporating) and on Caryl Churchill who was only able to produce half the play by the given deadline.

This half was a complete one-act play in itself: the section set in colonial Africa. I clearly remember settling down to read it with a mixture of excitement and trepidation and then an hour later putting it down with new feelings, delight and surprise: delight, because it was so successful as a sustained piece of cartooning, very funny, very sharp, and at the last moment chilling; surprise, because it bore no direct resemblance to the workshop which had never dealt specifically with Victorian sexual politics. Caryl had obviously been inspired and nourished by the workshop, but had then taken a bold imaginative leap and used a different period and society to highlight the themes of sexual prejudice and role-playing. She had also devised a brilliant way of forcing the audience to challenge their own preconceptions as we had ourselves done during the workshop: she wrote into the cast-list that the wife, Betty, should be played by a man, the black servant be played by a white, the son by a woman, and the daughter by a dummy which could be carelessly tossed around as the cute but negligible object the Victorians would regard a female offspring.

When the second act arrived it turned out to be considerably less successful. The central couple from Act 1, Clive and Betty, had grown old, returned to present day England, and retired to a bungalow on the coast. On a wet and cold weekend they are visited by their children with accompanying spouses and lovers and the piece focussed on the parents' inability to adjust to a modern permissive society. Part of the problem was that this theme had already been dealt with in Act 1, and more adventurously, as the Victorians did battle with the promiscuity of their human instincts. After a lengthy company meeting about Act 2, during which Caryl bravely and patiently suffered the ordeal of her baby being subjected to group molestation and battering, it was agreed all round that she should go away and rewrite it completely. In the meantime we would continue rehearsals of Act 1 where the writing was near-perfect and hardly required so much as a comma to be moved.

Within a remarkably short time Caryl produced a new and improved second act now set in a London park and now clearly a descendant of the workshop with its central characters our own generation, with monologues reminiscent of our life stories and a silent gay pick-up reminiscent of the card games. Although still very different in style to Act 1 it related more than its predecessor had; now there were occasional visitations by the Victorians in the form of ghosts and also one remnant of the cross-casting notion, with the monstrous tomboy Cathy to be played by a man.

Although improved, it still seemed to me unable to match the brilliance and originality of the first act or to relate to it with sufficient cohesion. I argued that Caryl should go away and try one last version, but was duly outvoted. It was not till years later that I was to realise how wrong my judgement had been, so it is fortunate at the time that my cries of dissent went unheeded and rehearsals proceeded.

We opened at Dartington College on the 14 February 1979, proceeded to have a very successful tour, and then in London, despite unenthusiastic reviews, played to packed houses. Still privately convinced that we only had half a play, I attributed this success to the presence in the cast of a star name, Julie Covington, who also happened to be a fine actress. So I continued to watch perplexed as the play travelled across the Atlantic, opened on Broadway with an American cast, and became even a bigger success there.

Then a year later Max revived the production at the Royal Court with a new British cast and finally I could view the play objectively. It was a revelation. The first act was indeed delightful, but the real strength and heart of the piece lay correctly in Act 2. The main pleasure for me was seeing how well it all worked together after all, and how like the experience of the original workshop watching it was: a gradual accumulation of understanding, a widening of horizons, a celebration of being human. I realised I had been judging it too analytically; its power in action is to open its arms wide to an audience and embrace everyone, theatre operating half-way between group therapy and a religious service, comforting, uniting, uplifting an audience; theatre at its most emotional and least intellectual, which is why, I suppose, it had not been a great hit with the critics. The Americans have a phrase for what a play like *Cloud Nine* does – it hits you where you live.

I wonder why I found *Cloud Nine* so much more satisfying as an audience than as a member of the cast. Perhaps my judgement of Act 2 had been subconsciously affected by the fact that I had only been given a small (but delightful) part in it, that of Cathy. One of the hardest disciplines when working for Joint Stock is keeping separate one's interests as actor and as company member. There are enormous advantages in working for the company, not least being able to share the responsibility for all artistic and administrative decisions, but there are also limitations, I think, for both the writer and the actor. All Joint Stock plays are ensemble pieces, written with equal parts for everyone. This is obviously a limiting form – it is no accident that most of the great plays, classical and modern, have at their centre one or two large roles whose journey the audience can follow. I have an appetite for these kinds of roles and so in the end I suppose I'm not really a Joint Stock actor. All the same, in a non-professional capacity I remain eternally grateful for what I learned during that workshop and, as an audience member, eternally grateful for the play that it produced.

Carole Hayman (actress)

Then there was . . .

Tramping across the frozen fields on Dartmoor in a morale boosting exercise with a cast of terrified actors who had a first night the following day and a couple of scenes of *Cloud Nine* still not written.

Pleurisy in Dublin.

My aunt leading the laughter with a whooping hoot that had all the actors corpsing on a sparse night in Edinburgh.

Doing *Cloud Nine* with half a set in Hull.

Groupies. Much competition amongst the men for the dirtiest story they could tell of them. One longed for the return of the unisex dressing-room.

Nylon sheets. Uugh.

Arguments about actors' rights. If they contributed to the play shouldn't they get some of the royalties?

Getting angry about 'actions'.

Richard Wilson (director)

The House
The 'house' in question was one of many private residences taken over for the care of wounded 'Tommies' during the 1914-18 war. These mini-hospitals were mainly staffed by middle and upper-class women known as VAD's (Voluntary Aid Detachments). They had no previous domestic or medical experience and certainly had never come into contact with working-class men before. They came under the direct control of the nurses.

We researched the subject from every angle – the background and causes of the war, the class structure of the time – we talked to old VAD's and old soldiers alike, to anyone who had lived through the period and we listened to historians and sociologists. As well as all the talking and reading, the men drilled, dug trenches and gradually began to build characters who knew what regiments they were in, where they had fought and where they were wounded physically and geographically. The women rolled bandages, scrubbed floors, learned the basic skills of dressing wounds, how to do 'hospital corners' and worked out who their characters were and how they were placed in society.

All this was building up to a long improvisation at the end of the workshop period in which the actors would spend virtually an entire day in character –in 'the house'. This particular '1916 day' duly arrived and everyone went about their business: early morning tea was served, dressings were changed, the men got out of bed and some helped the staff with the preparation of lunch. A VAD and a soldier were sent out to buy provisions – in character. The author (David Halliwell), the assistant director (Danny Boyle) and myself became ghost-like moderators – we could go where we liked, listen and observe and no one would so much as look at us.

The morning took its course: here a nurse helped a disabled man to read, over there laughter rippled from the kitchen as lunch began to take not only shape but smell. The work seemed to have paid off; one began to feel like a privileged eavesdropper on a day in a country at war in 1916. A strong sense of the period was evolving.

As lunch got even closer, Danny Boyle was sent out into the London of 1979 to buy some sorely needed knives and forks. Being a good 'Joint Stocker', he got the cheapest he could find – some rather strange silvery plastic objects with wooden handles. Lunch was served and, as I remember it, because of some celebration that day the women and the men ate together. Before they sat down, however, Sister directed that meals be sent to the three tradesmen in the ante-room. The ghostly observers had taken on minor roles to avoid starvation. I don't remember eating much of the proferred lunch, not only because I wanted to watch 'them' eat but because the concoction tasted truly awful.

No one dared mention this at the table, of course. Although a celebration was taking place, each side knew its boundaries. The atmosphere was slightly strained, the pecking order well maintained. The odd respectable joke was floated and the laughter was polite and contained. A sense of place and time was achieved, helped no doubt by St Gabriel's Hall in Pimlico which was built around that period. However, the atmosphere was broken rather suddenly when one of the newly acquired knives split into two pieces. The wooden handle wasn't in fact a handle – it was a biro pen! For a moment danger loomed. The whole improvisation was about to slip into the seventies. But with great aplomb, the actors opened out the situation and carried on through lunch with their biro-knives and forks well into the afternoon.

Although my memory is not all that accurate – and I certainly don't wish to be quoted – I think I remember two lines of dialogue from the lunch that didn't get into the final play:–

Soldier: Excuse me miss, my knife has turned into a funny sort of pen!

VAD: I don't think we really wish to know that Robinson. Eat your lunch.

Pauline Melville (actress)

In *An Optimistic Thrust*, we abandoned the sociological approach that had become almost traditional with Joint Stock and decided to use improvisation and mask work as part of the show itself rather than aids to the final production. We were provided with a vast array of costumes and props that allowed the work to take off in a sensual and imaginative direction rather than an analytical one. We endeavoured to look to our own histories, beliefs and influences – what had haunted or inspired us – convinced that as products of this society such an exploration would lead us to present some vision of it.

The work soon became a journey into surrealism. One day Bill Gaskill asked us each to create, from our personal histories, a 'ghost' that would represent the pressures and influences that had shaped us. I remember David Rintoul's 'ghost'. He built a wide passageway with screens and placed lit candles at regular intervals along it. On one side another actor was in bed representing David as a child. Dressed as a craggy old man, David slowly approached the bed from the far end of this eerie corridor intoning an endless list of academic qualifications – doctorates from various universities, the colours of their gowns. He ended with a recitation of Dunbar's *Lament for the Makaris* – 'Timor mortis conturbat me'. It was a compelling piece of theatre. I remember Julie Covington's 'ghost'. She had divided herself lengthwise to create a schizophrenic character, half-schoolgirl, half-tart. Later, I think, she changed it to a woman with a corpse-like dummy strapped to her back. Day after day work was done that I remember more vividly now than many plays I have seen since.

As we began to work with masks, more extraordinary characters arrived with bizarre obsessions and unthwartable drives. Improvisations were often hilarious. Paul Jesson created a woman called Mrs S.V., a jolly, portly woman who was always trying to recommend some cheap brand of cure-all medicine or to fuck the Duke of Edinburgh – sometimes both at the same time. We took characters from literature that had influenced us and added them to the melting pot. One long improvisation took place in the Minotaur's labyrinth. You never knew who was coming round the corner as each actor changed in and out of the characters they had created. Miss Havisham might meet and play a scene with Don Quixote; Mrs S.V., in her search for the Duke of Edinburgh, might find herself a puzzled witness to the final battle of Theseus and the Minotaur.

It was like a dream, a wild carnival procession; but somehow we did not manage to harness this cavalcade and transform it into an accessible play. It was, indeed, an optimistic thrust that somewhat missed its mark. But as George Devine would have said, artists should have the right to try and to fail.

Nick Darke (writer)

As the playwright responsible for Joint Stock's biggest critical disaster in its twelve year history, I don't feel qualified to write about the company's success, but I went through the famous 'process', got an enormous lot out of it, and enjoyed nearly every minute of it. We all worked well together and, whereas the workshop period in our case was not to do with researching the material for the play, (an element I regret) we certainly got to know each other well, and this paid huge dividends later, when the going got tough.

I remember sitting around in a circle, (a device, now common, but pioneered by Joint Stock, it must be remembered) in the rehearsal room at the Riverside Studios, on the day the first draft of my play was read. We had all met for the first time together after a break of six weeks from intensive workshops, and only I amongst all of us had been working – writing. The play was a mess and they told me so, all of them, I seem to remember, though that is probably an exaggeration. I was humiliated, without dignity and terrified. I got little sympathy from a group of actors, a director, and a musical director who were committed to touring this rubbish round the country for three months, whilst I sat at home waiting for the royalties.

We worked and worked on the play during the six week rehearsal period with an intensity I haven't indulged in before or since. I don't think a word of the final draft wasn't mine, but the feeling of combined effort and commitment by the whole company made the product something special for all of us, and when I meet anyone now, five or six years later, who was involved with the production, we speak of it and our compadres with warmth and affection.

We liked the play. More than that, they enjoyed performing it and I enjoyed watching it. Speaking for myself that is another phenomenon almost unique to my experience.

It was a baptism of fire for me, a collective creation which worked, and who cared if it was beaten to death by the critics? I did. I don't now, but I did then, I think we all did, the critical reaction made me ill and angry and despondent and paranoid. No account had been taken of the process which had brought about this wierd little piece, no one had bothered to question how the sweat had mingled in a unique, mysterious way to form this awkward drop, which somehow proved too salty for everyone's taste but our own.

I suppose in many people's eyes we had failed, but I don't see that play as a failure, I can't speak for the others. I suppose if we all got together and did another one, the same team, a few years older and wiser, there are strictures we would all make as a result of lessons learned. The only one for me would be that we choose our subject matter more carefully, that it is something that I, the writer, know a great deal about, and we spend at least half our workshop period, if not more, researching the specific topic about which I will be called upon to write, so we begin the process of working on the play collectively before it is written. That would be a wonderful way to write a play.

Deborah Findlay (actress)

Whenever I think of *Borderline* I think of David Beames with his red hair, and me in my salwar kamis playing Asian parents and radical separatists. It was a totally absorbing acting exercise. Having previously played a German, an Irish and an Italian woman, there should have been no difference in playing an Asian. But, of course, politically, there was. Some people found the result exciting. Others were horrified. For them the casting simply reflected the racist attitudes the play was trying to expose. All Joint Stock plays are in one way or another the product of the particular group assembled for the workshop. The earnestness, the humour, the naivety work their way through into the final production.

The company assembled for the project was a fair cross-section of actors: three blacks, three whites, three men, three women. However, it soon became clear none of us had any real knowledge of the subject in hand. So we became researchers, coming back to the rehearsal room (we moved our base to Southall) to show each other who we had met, and improvising around their lives. We assumed the role of a benevolent, non-racist enquirer, probing into the 'Asian problem', a group persona that was portrayed in the play as an ambitious journalist researching a documentary about racism. As it turned out, the real problem was that, as a group, we never confronted our own racism.

As work progressed, I realised that as we were only researching Asians there was a possibility of white actors playing black characters. The precedent of cross-casting was talked about. If the play took the form of a picaresque with everyone playing everything – blacks whites, women men and vice versa – the problem would disappear. But it didn't turn out that way. With the play written, the group committed to the project and excited about rehearsals, the absence of any exploration of our own attitudes to racism left us unprepared to handle the problem. The choices were stark: should David and I resign and upset the cohesion of the group? Or should we honour our commitment to the production? Other actors had told me that the only way to work with Joint Stock is to give yourself wholeheartedly to the process. If you don't relish the idea of the meetings, the research, the arguments about the play, don't accept the offer. I think this is true. But *Borderline* was a difficult journey.

Rita Wolf (actress)

Borderline was Joint Stock's nineteenth production and yet the first to employ non-white actors. It started life as a project about Britain's immigrant community – the next stage, if you like, in British imperialist history. Three of the actors chosen for the workshop were of Indian descent: Vincent Ebrahim, who was brought up in South Africa; Nizwar Karanj, brought up in Bombay; and myself, born, only just, in Calcutta but otherwise from north London.

Our researches led us to the Indian/Pakistani community now resident in Southall – 'little India' as it is known to the locals. It had, even at that time, become very well established. Shops, advice centres, 'hang-outs' where you could guarantee finding only brown faces, turbans and 'cockney-Hini' were all thriving. Having reached a degree of familiarity with our subject, actually finding people who bore out the research was very exciting. Specific types of dress and dialect, the wholesale import of the caste system received understanding nods from the group. We were boldly going where no middle-scale touring theatre group had gone before. But as we attempted to take our discoveries out onto the streets of Southall, hoping somehow to create a play from the combination of the two, we found waiting round the corner – racism. Pure and simple. There it was, the wall you walked into every time anyone took you into their confidence. How could we bandy aesthetics with these people? All I could hear were cries for help from people whose lives were being destroyed by the activities of white racists. I felt terrible. I think we all did, disgusted to be so ignorant of what was happening under our very noses. Our focus had to shift from something exotic and distant to survival on the streets of London.

Determined to keep the show positive, to highlight the resilience and wit of the immigrant community in the face of such adversity, we separated for the gap, each to have adventures of our own. That summer came with a bang. Spontaneous street warfare erupted in Toxteth, Bristol and Southall. The question that puzzled many people was why Asians – normally a peaceful, industrious social group – should suddenly freak out. What was widely dismissed as just another race riot, we had the inside information on. Southall people had finally had enough and were hitting back at the indiscriminate attacks and fascist marches that had been intimidating them for years. I was calm as I read the 'mad Asian bomber' headlines. I knew that a more topical show than ours could not be imagined. I had that old crusading feeling again.

We reconvened to find Hanif had produced a script that involved and engaged us all. Set in Southall, the central character was a teenage Pakistani girl from a strict Muslim background. Her gradual politicisation was the thread which bound the story together. (I was told before we reconvened that I would be playing the part.) Hanif had managed to incorporate in the play everything we had given him as well as the recent headline stories. With a bold stroke, we cast two of our three white actors in Asian roles. There was only one principal white character in the play. Still, we were Joint Stock. Everyone knew that with Joint Stock adults play children, men play women. So, for the first time, white would play black. The fact that none of our three black actors would be seen as white characters was something the company would doubtless rectify next season.

As soon as it opened, *Borderline* was branded controversial. It had Pakistani teenagers – of both sexes – openly discussing sex, petrol cans seen as a possible solution to the problem of racist attack, and the whole idea of integration was severely criticised throughout the text. It was a complex play, as complex as the facts we had uncovered while researching. Looking back, it is not the sensational tag that I am angry about. All the things *Borderline* said first were crying out to be said. What still infuriates me is the way Joint Stock have failed to follow up on those heady ideals of 1981. The liberal stance we took as a company in the face of the hatred and panic on the streets at the time needs further comment.

It took an inordinate amount of time for non-white actors to find their way into a Joint Stock show. Even then, in all our game playing, in the characters we brought back to the rehearsal room, even in the life-histories we gave of ourselves, the British racist was ever the missing element. Although it became clear very quickly that we would have to attempt a play that would show the effects of racism on people's lives, the racist was never given a voice. We spent no time in considering how close that voice might be to any of ours, hence no time on the very important question of how we, as a group, should seek to come to terms with our own racism. True, we all felt terrible about the lives we were investigating and had to keep telling ourselves that we had the material for a glorious, positive show. But, lemming-like, we took the side of the victims. Actual, everyday relations between black and white were hardly touched on. Inevitably, any real racial confrontation was omitted from our finished work.

In view of the recent social upheavals, how could the casting be seen as anything other than racist? Unless we were prepared to put our money where our mouth was and follow up *Borderline* with a play involving blacks playing whites, our position was indefensible. The challenge was not taken up and the work remains to be viewed as milestone or folly. For me, it was my first professional engagement, a formative theatrical experience by which I will measure all others. That five years later I am unable to defend the casting of our show is sad. I wanted so hard to believe that admirable Joint Stock line 'Adults play children, men play women, white plays black and vice versa'. For on that rested my whole future as a performer. One needs to have that freedom in mind before setting out and I grabbed it like a beacon. To this day I have not been vindicated – but I am still, amazingly, not without hope.

Jack Shepherd (director)

The caption read: 'Its all in their heads!' or something like that, and underneath, as I remember it, there a series of highly contrasted black and white photographs; faces distorted with effort and concentration, flecked with sweat, hair flying as if in a wind, the musical instruments they held twisted by movements too fast for the camera into strange fan-like shapes. I read this somewhat sensationalised account of a jazz concert in a doctor's waiting-room when I was about ten or eleven years old. I was astonished to learn that they 'made up the music as they went along'. They *improvised*. I had gone willingly to classical concerts at Leeds Town Hall, I had listened to my dad singing Handel's *Messiah*, not *un*happily as I recall. I had heard Geraldo on the radio, I had even listened somewhat reluctantly to Palm Court trios at Whitby Spa pavillion, but I was drawn to the idea of jazz improvisation even before I'd heard the music. It seemed an impossibly difficult thing to do. Given that the musicians were able, on the spur of the moment, to actually *invent* music, how did they manage to fit it in with what the other people were doing? How dare they leave so much to chance? And above all what happened in those flashes of inspiration when something was suddenly conjured out of nothing?

This fascination with improvisation continued into adult life. As a part-time jazz musician in the early sixties. As an art student. As a drama student. As an actor. As an occasional member of Theatre Machine and so on. The idea of creating drama out of improvisation was a fascinating possibility. The problem was *how*.

I worked at the problem consistently for the next ten years and more, re-examining 'The Method', rediscovering the *commedia dell'arte*, sharing ideas with, among others, Richard Wilson and Mike Leigh – who was as neat and naturalistic at that time as I was expressionistic and uncontrolled; until eventually a method of work began to emerge. The idea was *not* to impose on the actors, but to draw out the drama from *their* experience, from their dreams and associations, from the collective imagination. To create a play about our society and to *discover* a point of view as the work progressed.

It was a project based entirely on this process that I offered to the Joint Stock committee in the autumn of 1980. The struggle to get the project accepted was, I gathered later, rather acrimonious. I have only a vague idea of what took place; applicants are not told the content of the committee meetings where their projects are discussed, which is perhaps as well, but such was the stormy nature of the debate that I couldn't help but form an impression. I gathered that 'improvisation' was a contentious issue within Joint Stock, with a not altogether happy history. I also gathered that an actors' faction was broadly speaking *for* my idea and a writers' faction more or less *against* it. This surprised me. I didn't feel the idea was particularly controversial and I couldn't understand why the writers felt so threatened. But then, as someone told me later by way of reassurance, 'they always do'. In the end, after meetings that would have done the Quakers proud, my project was accepted; this left me with quite a lot to prove.

The workshop was scheduled for the autumn of 1981, which looked like clashing with the run of a compacted version of *Julius Caesar* and *Anthony and Cleopatra*, in which I was contracted to play Anthony, at the Mermaid Theatre. I worried about being over-committed. The problem was solved when I was sacked by Bernard Miles after three weeks of rehearsals. 'You're too much of a Geoff Boycott,' he said. 'What I want is an Ian Botham!' This cleared my head wonderfully.

I don't enjoy casting. It makes me feel like a slave owner, picking slaves. So I tried selecting the company through workshops, which gave the actors a fighting chance, and made me feel a whole lot better.

The workshop period was exhilarating, all ten weeks of it. There was a daily flow of energy, ideas, characters, commitment, hilarity, misery, bad temper, frustration, inertia, and so on. The acting company included in the early stages, the set designer, the stage management, the musical director. The idea was to involve everyone!

Some of the improvisations were perfect in themselves, but led nowhere. We didn't touch on anything that could be agreed on as a *theme*. But the work was rich in possibilities . . . Once the actor had decided on a narrative, he or she set about improvising the central character of that narrative in a series of scenes. Each actor, then, had a *leading* role in their own story, and *subsidiary* roles in the stories of others. A record was made of every improvisation, usually just a sentence or two in a note-book, and, after six weeks or so, I had an extraordinarily varied collection of scenes, but no readily available *form*, into which to mould them. There were eight people in the company, and potentially therefore, eight plays. This represented a real crisis, in the sense that it would have been possible at this stage to have selected the most *resonant* narrative and dropped the rest. This solution may well have produced the best drama, but the pursuit of it would have seemed like a betrayal. When people have invested their own experience in the construction of a play, it's always possible for the director to *alter* it, but not to reject it altogether. The alternative was to give each narrative equal weight and weave all the stories together until a new pattern emerged. This was the road we took.

Interestingly, a year later, I saw Kurosawa's film *Dodeska Den*, where the lives of people living in a Japanese shanty town are similarly threaded together. I found the film satisfying on many levels, the acting, and above all, the form. It was nice to watch the film and feel that I'd travelled – if only for a little way – down the same road.

Improvisation functions best when it is only lightly constrained. It was not possible therefore, in my opinion, to improvise the play night after night; either the repetitions would destroy it, or else it would break free from its restraints and become something else. The next stage in the process involved taping the improvisations, writing them down and whenever necessary, restructuring them. This was a frustrating and difficult process. Tempers shortened and, in the kitchen of the rehearsal room, tears were shed.

It was not evident what the play was about until after the first run through. It could be argued now, that it was about alienation, social, sexual, political, produced by an uncaring, greedy society; but it wasn't quite so clear at the time. At least it was funny, we were all agreed on that, and the acting was good.

In the main, the play flourished on tour and wilted a little in London. We were evidently outside the fashionable mainstream. *Real Time* turned out to be a play that was not overtly 'about something', about Northern Ireland, say, or homelessness, or world peace. Nor did it fit in with the popular notion that Joint Stock is in some vague sense a left wing, well, pinkish, theatre group. Nevertheless, it contained within it, in the long central scene in the art gallery, a particularly satisfying metaphor for the workings of capitalism.

A feeling still persists that we missed out on something. But what? If a camel is a horse designed by a committee, maybe we created a camel. Perhaps the ICA was the wrong London venue, in that the audience in residence expected something more overtly avant-garde. An interesting fact about experimental theatre is that it often employs *traditional* attitudes to rehearsal in order to produce *avant-garde* results. *Real Time* was quite possibly the reverse.

Jennie Stoller (actress)

We spent two weeks living in a cottage in Upwell in the heart of the Fens. There were eight of us, sometimes nine, and not enough beds. Imelda Brown had to sleep on the landing, Bernard Strother on the sitting-room floor. We were there to find out about the people of the Fens but we also found out a great deal about each other. Few of us had worked together before. Unlike other workshops we
did not go our separate ways at the end of the day so there was an added intensity to the work. We cooked together, read together, combed the village for people, stories, ideas, images – and fought like mad to get into the bathroom.

We had a list of people we wanted to talk to – land workers, church leaders, teachers, children – though we were initially quite apprehensive about whether they would want to talk to us. It proved relatively easy. Upwell is a small village. The people are not used to actors wandering the streets asking a lot of questions. ('Hullo. We're with a theatre group . . .'; 'You never are. Well, well!') Many were intrigued, others simply glad of the company and the chance to have a chat. It is a bleak, isolated place. One Saturday, four of us paid a lunchtime visit to the local pub. As I was buying a round, a man looked at me along the bar. 'You're a *Guardian* woman, aren't you?' I laughed. I had no idea what he was talking about. He followed me back to our table, took one look at the others and announced, 'You're all *Guardian* women.' He seemed both surprised and delighted. When we finally realised what he meant, he confessed he was the only person in the whole of Upwell who didn't read the *Mail* or the *Telegraph*. He was a *Guardian* reader and proud of it. His pleasure at finding four like minds in his local was only qualified by a lingering anxiety about who we were. 'Where you from? Outer Space?' He sat down, cupped his hands round his pint. 'Wherever I go in the village you're talking to people on the bridges or in the shops. There must be sixteen of you. What are you *doing*?'. We told him and, whatever he had imagined, the news that we were researching a play didn't come as a disappointment. He began to tell us his life story. 'Lord Melchett and me are the only Marxists in the Fens . . .'

The life he described was wholly unexpected. The black sheep of a Tory family, he had fought and won two industrial tribunals, been ostracised by the village on several occasions, and now worked a small orchard. His story was cut short when the pub closed but later that night he turned up at the cottage clutching a battered suitcase full of newspaper cuttings about the tribunals. Out of this encounter came material which Caryl used for the character of Nell.

Everyone we met had a story to tell or suggestions about who we ought to visit. ('Oh, you want to talk to Tony, my sugar. Runs the goldfish stall at the fair.') And there was always a surprise around the corner. One old woman in a red cardigan waved at Caryl through the window so some of us went in. She talked about her husband's death, her loneliness and a ninety-year-old woman whose father had been a chemist. He used to make opium pills for the poor people to 'cheer them up a bit'. Another woman talked about her convalescence after a major operation. She was lying in bed waiting for her husband to prepare a meal. He eventually appeared with a tin of pineapple and a can opener and asked her to open it for him as he didn't know how.

In the second week, four of us spent a day fruit-picking for a local farmer. We started at eight o'clock in the fog and the wet and finished at five, warmed by the effort and some late sunshine. The farmer insisted on paying us. The standard piece rate was 40p a bushel and we earned £8. It was hard, back-breaking work but invaluable when it came to re-creating the work scenes in rehearsal. To perfect these, Les set up an improvisation during the third week of the workshop back in London. Equipped with buckets of water, we had to move up and down the floor dabbing each wooden block. As soon as we had finished, we were told to go back and start again. We quickly discovered which muscles you need to be a potato picker and what it is to hate your boss. I've never looked at a bag of crisps in quite the same way ever since.

Other improvisations and exercises were devised to analyse the raw material we had gathered in the Fens. In reporting back our findings while we were in Upwell we had acted out the people we met, narrated their stories, described their posture, their clothes. Les and Caryl wrote everything down in little black books. Now we began to explore the underlying social relationships. One exercise involved a farmer and a farmworker. The worker wanted a wage increase but the farmer insisted on paying the worker in kind. The more gifts he received, the more guilty the worker became about asking for more money. This improvisation led to Frank's exchange with Mr Tewson in the play. Another exercise involved completing a set of physical tasks in a limited space of time. In turn, each of us had to iron a shirt, peel potatoes, sweep the floor, fold a sheet, feed a baby, settle a miserable child and give a man his tea. All in ten minutes. The women we had met in the Fens seemed to do everything – work in the field, organise the home, bring up the children – and as we summarised our impressions at the end of the workshop it was their experience that had left its mark on us all. Caryl's first idea for the title of the play was *Strong Girls Always Hoeing*, not a popular choice among the group but it fixed the monotony and the drudgery we had witnessed.

Several weeks into the tour of the production, one of the people we had met in the nearby town of Chatteris came to see the show. Sadly, we never played in the Upwell area – there was nowhere to perform – but Mrs Parrish made the journey to the nearest venue to see what we had come up with. Her husband came with her and when we asked him afterwards what he thought, he turned to Cec Hobbs and said, 'You had your hoe the wrong way round.' The mistake was soon corrected and the process that began so many weeks before in a cramped cottage came full circle. If there is one supreme virtue in the Joint Stock method I would say it is the opportunity to get at the detail – and the chance to get it right.

Lynda Farran (administrator)

10.00 a.m. A damp January morning. Two thousand pounds in cash in my Sainsbury's carrier bag and I'm off down the escalator to the south-bound tube and on the wages run destined for *Victory*. Having successfully avoided any potential mugger, I arrive at rehearsals to pay the wages of the company and to hear from them the progress of the project. Just time to give them an update on their tour schedule and what's happening with all the various committees and subcommittees before retreating back to my garret in Tottenham Court Road. A short meeting with the accountants to finalise the quarterly returns and just a few stage management to interview with the stage management committee, before embarking on my regular task of writing, typing and circulating the minutes from the last policy committee meeting; and another typical day comes to an end.

On my first day as general manager I arrived at Tottenham Court Road and climbed the three flights of stairs to find a totally deserted office. All it seemed that remained of Joint Stock was the memorabilia of past triumphs, photographs and posters on the walls from *Cloud Nine*, *Fanshen*, *The Speakers* and *The Ragged Trousered Philanthropists*. There was even a paint-brush in a glass frame! Files of old publicity material and scripts from the Joint Stock bookshop cluttered the floor and coffee cups and ashtrays littered every surface. The big problem was where to start. The general manager was the only full-time employee. After three days of hoovering and cleaning windows, and polishing the paintbrush (I had to do something) I found myself in my first meeting and things began to look up.

It was quite difficult to get to grips with the fact that, for a few months of the year when no show was on, Joint Stock comprised a small core of six past members, and for the rest of the year a fluctuating group of between six and forty members, often first-time and short-term. The new recruits very often found it difficult to grasp that they were simultaneously employer and employee and were responsible for the future policy and direction of the company. Progress in meetings was consequently painfully slow, while the 'regulars' initiated new members in the intricate rituals of management.

At an early meeting I was rapped over the knuckles by Max Stafford-Clark for issuing letter contracts to the actors. I had innocently thought that if the idea was for us to all improve our working conditions, it would be a step forward to let everyone have a written agreement of their terms and conditions of employment. Apparently not.

My role within the group was an initiator, financial advisor, and co-ordinator, and perhaps manipulator. The trust and responsibility given to me as general manager to administer the affairs of the group on their behalf was both daunting and challenging and I knew that with such an unwieldy management team, the responsibility for making the administration work was ultimately mine.

Arts Council drama officers would come and go, each one in turn being subjected to groups of vociferous directors, actors and stage management arguing for six-week rehearsal periods. I'm sure the officers would toss a coin on receiving an invitation to a Joint Stock meeting and it would be the loser who would have to attend!

New Year's Eve 1982 was a memorable occasion. The Joint Stock members, largely comprised of those touring *Fen* and those about to rehearse *Victory*, assembled at the Almeida Theatre. The issue for discussion: the production budget for *Victory*. In those days we had been operating within budgets of about £4,000 for a set. Director Danny Boyle together with designer Deirdre Clancy had come up with the most magnificent set, but it cost £9,500 – more than twice our usual budget. This kind of expenditure was unprecedented and would, I argued, put the company into deficit. Discussion carried on until about 10.30 p.m., four and a half hours later, when the expenditure was given approval. Although decisions were normally reached by consensus, I had to have it minuted that I could not agree. My argument was that the deficit would have to be paid off, at least in part, during the next financial year. The increased expenditure would not penalise the immediate productions, as expenditure was committed, and therefore not the majority of those attending the meeting – but it would be detrimental to future projects, perhaps mean employing one less actor, or losing a further rehearsal week. But, the meeting was fully aware of the implications of decisions. These were the rules, and I had to carry out the majority decision. As I remember, that was the only occasion when I was in disagreement with the majority. Had it been a regular occurrence, particularly over financial matters, I would have found it impossible to carry out my role as representative of the company.

The Annual General Meeting was one of the most taxing times for the general manager. There was an enormous amount of work which had to be prepared, approved, typed and circulated to the entire membership of Joint Stock. It took weeks. One evening, at about 11.00 p.m., I was still copying the final sheet of the minutes which I had intended to post that night when the photocopier broke down. In desperation I started to take it to pieces in a mad attempt to mend it. In the early hours I had to admit defeat and went home thoroughly depressed leaving piles of paper amidst the wreckage of a Gestetner.

The day of the meeting itself was very important. There would be over 100 people there, and I felt as if I was stepping on stage to give a performance before a *very* critical audience as I shuffled my papers and prepared to deliver the accounts. Questions and lively discussions usually ensued but it was always the more domestic issues like touring in an uncomfortable minibus or playing Edinburgh in winter which seemed to take precedence over more weighty matters of company finance.

All in all, despite the frustrations, my first impression was the right one. Joint Stock gave me a rare and much cherished opportunity to be involved in the process of playmaking.

Carole Hayman (director)

And I won't forget . . .

An early Christmas dinner in the White Horse Hotel in Barnsley. Five courses for £7. The guilt with which four women hedonistically shovelled mince pies and wine. For we were on a fact-finding mission about the miners' strike and had spent all day discussing poverty.

Arriving in Bradford and finding a small box of a theatre with no wings at all for a play that had twenty-five scene changes with beds and three-piece suites.

Divali in Leicester. A huge room full of brilliant moving saris.

A chilly dark early morning in Yorkshire. A pit village perched high with twinkling lights on the surrounding moors. The sun coming up and glinting on rows and rows of policemens' shields.

Writer interviewed by eager journalist:

Journalist: Now. About your new play. The Great Celestial . . . (*Hasty glance at poster*) . . . Pig.
Writer: Cow!
Journalist: Pardon?!
Writer: Not you. The play.

An Indian woman of thirty crying as she told her life story. Was she crying because the story was awful? (It was.) No. Because no one had ever asked her before.

Ralph Brown (actor)

Blackpool. Monday afternoon, a wet October.
Six actors, a director and a writer meet each other in the lounge of the

Pendale Hotel (just off the town map) and plan their assault on the Labour Party Conference; the largest collection of journalists to be found outside of a Fleet Street pub. Our mission: to explore their world, their obsessions. We have (valued possessions) press passes saying 'Joint Stock' pinned to our clothing, currently providing simple entry to the Winter Gardens. We are naïve, optimistic, nervous, brave. We move in.

A fringe meeting upstairs from the bar is getting underway. Entrance is through a sea of leaflets thrusting at you from Nicaragua to the Kent coalfields. Inside, a large surreal Spanish galleon of a room is filling up. TV cameras at the front, lights. A sense of excitement. The speakers tonight are Livingston, Benn, Scargill. I am looking for journalists. What do they wear? How do they talk? Who do they vote for? Why are they journalists? Will they even talk to me? I see two, identifiable by their press passes, and sit down next to them, a youngish woman and an older, bespectacled man.

'Hello,' I offer boldly. 'Can I talk to you?' They look at me. I launch in. 'My name is Ralph Brown and I'm up in Blackpool with Joint Stock Theatre Group and we're researching a play about journalists and we don't know what it's about yet and can I talk to you?' They are both from *The Sunday Times*, covering the conference – she is on the Insight team, he is the local man in Lancashire.

'We set the agenda for this conference,' he claims. 'Three weeks ago our front page said Kinnock would be in trouble on three fronts at this conference – the police, the miners, the local authorities. And that's the way the conference will go.' He evidently felt that this was the legitimate role of the paper, but perhaps feeling he had said too much started to move away. 'Talk to Ros,' he said, 'she's the expert on the miner's strike.' Could I meet him later I asked, at the Imperial Hotel perhaps? He smiled and nodded and moved off. The woman grabbed my arm. 'Do you know who that is?' she whispered. '*He's* the one you want to talk to. That's Michael Jones, political editor of *The Sunday Times*.' I was going to have to be a little smarter over the course of the next three weeks. There was a stirring at the front of the hall. Scargill was entering – he timed it well, and the room erupted as their hero moved onto the platform. The feeling was quite extraordinary. Suddenly the press became noticeable leaning against walls, slouching in chairs, bored. Even so, notebooks were produced, pens from inside pockets, and attention brightened a little: the studied boredom of their poses couldn't quite smother the sense of history.

Later, the bar and foyer of the Imperial Hotel provided the true flavour of the conference. The place was full of journalists and politicians, and Joint Stock valiantly camouflaged within. Peter Hillmore (*Observer*) peered at my press pass suspiciously, exchanged a sentence with me and decided that there were more important people to talk to. Sir Robin Day was decidedly the worse for wear and tottering on the steps with a young woman in black. I cornered Mick Costello, industrial editor of the *Morning Star*, smoking cigars and hobnobbing happily with capitalist comrades from the *Telegraph* and *Express*. In fact there was an awful lot of hobnobbing going on. I think everyone there was drunk. I met Michael Jones again, he welcomed me with open arms, told me the play didn't have a hope of understanding 'the relationship between me and the office', confessed to always having had ambitions to being one of the opinion-forming elite, and wished me the very best of luck, young man.

'Of course it's very different when the Tories are here,' a wobbling hack confided. 'Last year it was wonderful though, Parkinson – you remember?' Little did he suspect that 'Tories' would provide the best story for a decade only ten days later.

It was Scargill's week, undoubtedly. Adulated by conference, hated and adored by the press, 'Coal Not Dole' stickers everywhere and buckets being rattled at every door. Quite a time. We all had our adventures. Simon Curtis followed a *Sun* reporter for one afternoon hoping to catch some juicy bit or other, and was spotted trying to listen in on a conversation. I was finally confronted by this man, a stocky Scot, who told me that if my friend didn't lay off he would receive a crack on the head. I talked to him. I was getting quite good at asking the right questions. He told me how he'd always wanted to be a policeman, and had fallen into journalism at a Spencer Davis concert in Glasgow.

The Joint Stock method meant that observation was crucial. Each morning we would present, one at a time, a character we had encountered the day before, with close attention to detail: accent, hand movements, figures of speech etc. Sometimes we would write notes. I found it easier and more accurate to rely on memory. If more than one of us had been there, we could present the group with a 'scene'. We slowly discovered which questions and lines of conversation gave the best 'results', but it was always the unexpected, the surprising, which caught the imagination of the group. It was for me a wonderfully exciting way to work.

My final memory of Blackpool was a *Daily Mirror* press conference called by Robert Maxwell to present a granny from Essex with a huge cheque for one million pounds. The scene was grotesque, and finally made it's way into *Deadlines* in all it's surreal horror, with myself playing the elephantine Maxwell. I remember the poor woman standing there, with cameras clicking, TV arc lights, microphones and questions, a glass of champagne glued in her hand, a frozen smile on her bewildered face. She turned to Marge Proops standing next to her and asked if it was all right for her to have a sip. Later, Kathryn Pogson and I spoke to her daughter. 'You're not from the *Sun* are you? We've been told not to answer any questions.' We explained that we were actors doing research and suddenly the woman recognised Kathryn: 'You were on TV weren't you?' She immediately relaxed and took us into her confidence. 'They've been ever so good. We've been to four hotels in four days. We had the phone call saying we'd won, and they said just pack a suitcase. We left the washing in the machine.' Her son was whimpering. 'Shut up,' said his dad, 'I've bought you loads of things today.' They had just won a million pounds. *Mirror* men were gently ushering people to a photocall with the trams. 'Let's just hope we've got more friends than enemies' was the daughter's final anxious thought, as Kathryn and I left for the Big Dipper.

The company left for Sheffield, the heart of the miners' strike, and spent two days at the local paper; the *Morning Telegraph*, and the *Sheffield Star*, the evening paper which shared the same office, again asking questions and listening. I suggested to the industrial editor ('a close friend of Arthur' someone whispered) that being a local reporter was something of a luxury, being able to be accurate and honest and truthful. 'No,' he said, 'I just have to live here.' It was becoming increasingly difficult to parry the obvious question:

'What's the play about?' We really had no idea, and the people we talked to, especially the journalists, just couldn't accept this. 'You're going to expose us aren't you? All the drink and sex.' And in truth we were beginning to behave more and more like journalists: finding ways of making people talk, being persistent, looking for angles.

Simon Curtis and I visited some picket lines at Maltby and Silverwood collieries, and spent one afternoon talking to two miners who were on strike, one of whom, Jim, became a character in the play. Throughout the two and a half hour conversation, Simon had been fingering a five pound note in his pocket, preparing to give it to the fund before he left. 'Do you have a collection?' he asked the young miner. 'Sure, just give it to me, we'll mek sure it gets t' reght place.' Simon pulled out the note and offered it. They both looked at it. It was a twenty pound note. 'Oh,' said the miner. Simon's eyes glazed over. 'Oh thanks a lot,' said the miner. Simon's fingers released the note, and he smiled weakly. We drove off, Simon in a state of some shock.

The company then moved to the hustle and bustle of London, Fleet Street, the TV studios and radio stations. The journey was important. The people we had talked to 200 miles north were filtered and made into 'news' down here in the capital. Stephen Wakelam was particularly affected by this geographical change, and the play's sweep covers the quiet of the South Yorkshire countryside to the claustrophobic newsrooms of London. My favourite place was BBC *Newsnight*, 'We're doing a play about the media,' I offered as an introduction to Howard, sleeveless-jerseyed, *Guardian*-reading type. He swung round in his typical journalist's swing-round chair. 'Media!' He glared at me, managing to look totally harmless. 'Don't lump us in with the bloody *Express*, *Mirror* and *Beano*. This is a television news programme.'

Peter Snow had an SDP poster in the room where he was working. I desperately wanted to ask him if it was his, but couldn't find the words. It was very very difficult to ask journalists about their politics. They pretended not to have any. Or they said, 'I'm nosy' or 'I'm an observer'. Others were more approachable, notably those at the *Express* where a considerable number of the writers are members of the Labour Party! I was devastated by this disclosure, although the *Express* journalists I spoke to found it totally normal. 'It's the same at the *Mail*, the *Sun*, the *Telegraph*. You've got to earn a living.' I suggested the two things might be incompatible. 'I've never written a word against the Labour Party in twelve years on the *Express*.' The man seemed proud of this, as if his principles were still intact. Fiona Millar, one of the few women on the paper, had an even worse situation, surrounded by pin-ups and being given the Royal stories or the animal stories because of her gender. 'My generation is terribly disappointed in the profession we've joined,' she told me. She is late twenties, and moved from a local paper to Fleet Street just when it was going down the drain: bingo, tits and circulation wars. She was consoled by the fact that the *Express* was a 'writer's paper' rather than a subeditor's paper. Subeditors – the back bench – are a strange group of men (invariably) who sift the paras, reorganise the stories and, in many cases, rewrite according to the paper's politics.

The *Sun* was more difficult. We trooped up to the office and were told to wait by the door. We huddled there, feeling like intruders. A nervous face told us about 'the *Sun*' glancing over his shoulder now and again. One of us was escorted to the toilet and back. We were not allowed to talk to any journalists.

The face we were talking to had a plastic smile which it kept putting on to reassure us, and only succeeded in totally unnerving us. 'We are a family newspaper. We never print anything unless it's checked. We write for an average reading age of eight.' He did, however, tell us the name of the cabinet minister whom the whole of Fleet Street knew was fucking small boys. And somehow, this one rather sordid point was a believable oasis in the desert of his insincerity.

And so to the Tories. We took it in turns to visit the Tory Conference in Brighton, (only had two press passes) and Tricia Kelly and I found ourselves on the train down just hours after an IRA bomb had wrecked the Grand Hotel. There was security everywhere. The atmosphere inside the conference hall was extraordinary. Resilience, survivors. Thatcher got an emotional standing ovation just for being there. Tricia and I felt like enemies of the people in the midst of the mob, protected by the legitimate neutrality of our press passes. It meant we didn't have to applaud. We could look cool and detached and professional. This was a relief. Thatcher was finally introduced, as a 'great statesman' and she spoke for the whole hall about Tebbit's bravery, property, owners and earners, and got a massive, absurd standing ovation at the end. Tricia and I made our way to the door and stopped to watch this display of political football hooliganism. We were ushered out by a rather embarrassed man, as if this was a private Tory moment not to be witnessed by the unfaithful.

We moved out onto the beach. The Grand Hotel had a huge hole knocked out of it, the beach was roped off, police were everywhere. Earlier, I had tried to have a few words with Simon Hoggart of the *Observer*, one of our contacts. 'Haven't got time,' he said, rushing away. 'Best story for twenty-five years.' There were journalists *everywhere*. Every paper and TV station had quintupled its Brighton staff. By now, we Joint Stockers were behaving like journalists ourselves, moving towards huddles of people instinctively for titbits, trading information, becoming strangely distanced from the event. The process was not dissimilar: the workshop, the story.

I remember the feeling standing on Brighton beach, so clearly. An exhilarating sense of history. It was all happening around me: the strike, the conferences, the bomb. I felt at the centre of the universe.